The Basics of Mysticism

Defining the Six Facets of Spiritual Development

The Basics of Mysticism

Defining the Six Facets of Spiritual Development

Mischa VAlyea

The Publisher: Aashni Spiritual Living

Kansas City, MO 64118

USA

Website: www.AashniSpiritualLiving.com

Email: info@AashniSpiritualLiving.com

ISBN: 0-9887312-7-4

ISBN-13: 978-0-9887312-7-1

PUBLISHER'S NOTE

This publication is designed to provide accurate and authoritative information in regard to the subject matter covered. It is sold with the understanding that the publisher is not engaged in rendering psychological or medical services. If expert counseling or medical assistance is needed, the services of a competent professional should be sought.

TABLE OF CONTENTS

Introduction
Demystifying the Mystery of Mysticism

I know why you are here. You have been bitten. Bitten by the bug to know the divine. You most probably have had an experience that was wondrous and you want to understand what happened and how to experience it again, on a regular basis. I know this because I was like you. I, too, had tasted the edge of a new world. But like you, I had no idea what this experience was or how to go about making it more than a fleeting glimpse of pure heaven. I listened to others describe their experiences. I read the works of the saints and the sages. I soaked in every possible viewpoint, from every religion that I could get my hands on, but it wasn't enough. I wanted to experience the divine for myself.

I asked every person I met if there was a of system of awakening. Everyone told me that mysticism is a *mystery*. It just unfolds and each person's awakening is unique. Nothing can be planned. The map of awakening draws itself as you advance. I became frustrated. In essence, they were telling me that I must recreate the wheel that all the previous mystics had created. On top of all this, there were ominous warnings that the results of transformation could be disastrous to one's physical and mental health. Surely, someone had discovered a universal roadmap and could guide me through the winding curves of transformation. What I wanted was an experience of peace and calm that I could call upon at will, not a bunch of intellectual arguments and debate.

As the sages foretold, my path has been unique. I have taken many wrong turns. I have experienced the heights of glory and the depths of despair. I have somehow survived pitfalls that turn the typical enthusiastic seeker into the cynical and disgruntled atheist. All the while, I learned about myself. I would not wish for my path to be different, but I have come to know that much of the difficulty I experienced along this winding road of personal development was completely unnecessary.

I know this because there is an overall structure to spiritual development. There is a method to the madness, because the mystery is a science.

Mysticism is the science of consciousness.

It is a realization that is so subtle that modern scientists have yet to develop methods to reveal it. It is perfectly understandable to describe mysticism as a *mystery*. The experiences of the mystics are indescribable and cannot be comprehended by the logical mind. When you add in the cultural beliefs and expressions of the intended audience, this makes the mystical texts quite unusual and very hard to grasp. But if mysticism is truly the science of consciousness, then it can't continue being described as a *mystery*. There is no scientist on this planet that will accept this flakey definition. Science demands structure and repeatability. To be considered a legitimate science, mysticism needs a concrete definition that is the catalyst for experimentation and study. My definition of mysticism is:

*Mysticism is the science of optimizing the body-mind-spirit complex
in a way that harmonizes the chemistry of the body,
the psychology of the mind,
and the bioelectrical field of the spirit
so that it beneficially transforms the human experience.*

Mystical science requires that the understandings be integrated because mysticism is multifaceted and these facets are interdependent. Changes to one facet of the matrix will affect the other facets as well. So, when you participate in a spiritual fast, it will affect the physical processes of the body. If you process through a psychological issue, it will allow the spiritual energies to flow more efficiently through the mind and body. If you set aside time to do rituals or practices that, too, will affect your overall experience.

Any theory of spirituality must be inclusive. It must harbor within it all belief systems and processes of personal transformation. Mysticism is universal. It is the goal of all religions. The only thing that differs between religions is the process of transformation. Regardless of religion, the mystic understands that there is only One True God. This god is consciousness itself. God is the "All in All" that is omnipresent, omnipotent, and omniscient. God is the expanse of space and not a Him or a Her. While you will need to practice a system that uses the duality of masculine and feminine to reach this wholeness, it is important to understand that this is just a vehicle, not the absolute. Once you become set in your thinking that god is either a male or a female, you have negated the system of balance by taking sides. The true mystic knows that each religion is striving to bring its followers to the exact same experience, which is balance. It is only from a position of balance that you can experience the expanse of consciousness.

You will not find a group of mystics arguing over theological doctrine. Once the divine expanse is found, the differences amongst the religions are the result of differing viewpoints. It is like seeing the Statue of Liberty. We know that all descriptions depend upon how a person or group viewed the statue. Did they fly over in a plane? Did they take a boat to the island? Did they ride up and down in the elevator and look out through the crown? Each experience is valid and true. For a mystic, they are all accepted regardless of whether the mystic has personally had that experience, because they know that each person is unique and any experience is the sum total of all previous experience.

Even though the experiences themselves are the same, translation is necessary to see the similarities between the philosophies. In this book, we will see that the Middle Eastern symbol for the energy that falls from the sky is bread. Wheat is the staple grain of the mid-eastern populations. The empires of Mesopotamia and Egypt relied upon the production of wheat, which is the foundation for making bread. This is why the breaking of bread is celebrated in the Abrahamic religions. The same experience in the Buddhist tradition, however, is symbolized by the eating of milk rice. The Asian world, even today, relies upon rice as its staple grain. Stories of the Buddha tell of him being saved from death by a young girl who brings him a bowl of milk rice. Both symbols, the bread and the milk rice, are eatable, white, and made of grains that are blessed by the water that falls from the sky. So, while they seem different, once we have translated the symbols, we find that they are just different ways to express the same experience.

While there are many truths, or laws, in mysticism, the prime tenant is balance. To reach the heights of joy and understanding requires that all three realms of the body-mind-spirit complex be in balance. Balancing the body, the mind, and the spirit is the science of mysticism. Balancing the body entails eating a proper diet, getting enough exercise, and taking time to rest. Developing the weaker brain circuits and processing past traumas and issues balances the mind. Building the spiritual energies, through practices and rituals, will allow you to handle the stresses of life with ease.

While there are three realms to mysticism, the mystical writings place the highest emphasis on balancing the energies that are found in the realm of the spirit. There are two divine energies within the spiritual system. These two energies are:

The Water energy, which falls from the sky, brings Peace.
This energy was known as the Divine Masculine Energy in antiquity.

The Fire energy, which rises up from the earth, brings Love.
This energy was known as the Divine Feminine Energy in antiquity.

Unlike the monotheistic system, which implies that one energy is bad and the other energy is good, this twofold system seeks balance between these opposites. In a two-fold energy system, neither energy is considered bad or good in and of itself. We will be incorporating the same philosophy used by Taoists when they explain the relationship between the yin and yang. It is the interplay between these two energies that creates the bioelectrical field of the soul.

The dynamic blending of these two energies is very subtle. It is hard to determine if you have achieved a balanced state because the human bioelectrical field cannot be measured at this time. One way to judge the state of the energies is to notice change in the realms of the body and the mind. When the energies in the spiritual system are strengthened, the need to eat and sleep becomes less. This is why the proof of attainment is many times related to how much a person eats or sleeps. There have been reports of many saints who go years without eating. In most recent times, the Buddha boy gained massive notoriety when he sat under a tree without eating or drinking for months on end. Energy science, like acupuncture, energy healing, and reiki - when administered correctly - can heal the body. The flow of the energies can also wipe away mental issues and traumas.

The mystical path is a process of gradual change. Your lifelong issues and personal habits need to be addressed gradually so that you do not put unnecessary stress on yourself. Drastic change upsets the balances. Since the facets are interdependent, unbalance in one facet can cause great harm in the other facets. Like a scuba diver, who must go slowly so that they can adjust to the pressures of the ocean, the mystic must descend and ascend gradually. Jumping in and changing everything all at once will destroy, not just the health, but also the desire to continue with the program. Have you ever decided that you need to get fit? Then, gone to the gym and completed an extreme workout? What was the result? Most likely you experienced so much pain and stiffness that you did not return to the gym for many weeks, if ever again. It is best to experience growth gradually. This way your life improves with the least number of setbacks.

THEORY VS PRACTICE

Mystical transformation is a paradox. Mysticism is more than an intellectual philosophy that can be read in a book and tested with an exam. It is an experience.

*The mystical texts are telling you what it **feels** like to travel the path of transformation.*

You must practice to understand the theory. But, you must understand the theory before you are able to select the correct practice. All the philosophical arguments are just dust if you do not practice. Until you have experienced the *feeling* of being on fire without being burned, you will not understand the mystical writings. If you limit yourself to reading books and listening to gurus, you will not experience the realizations that are required to transform your being.

On the other side of the spectrum, every religion and spiritual practice is valid in the scheme of consciousness, but the real question is, "Is this practice right for *you*?" We are all unique individuals. What is best for one person is not what is best for everyone. Enlightenment comes from following a path that that deals with *your* issues and is compatible with *your* personality.

A spiritual plan is like selecting a destination on a road map. You cannot say you want to be transformed and then do nothing. You have to know the destination of where you want to go. Once the destination is selected, it is still impossible to chart a path to that destination until you know your beginning point. Outside of the relationship between two points, a map is just a pretty picture. It is important to decipher where you are in relation to where you want to go. This will determine the direction of travel.

Let's say the destination selected is Los Angeles. Until you have established where you are in relation to this destination, it is impossible to select a route that will lead you to this location. So, let's say you are located in New York City. The shortest and most direct route from New York City to Los Angeles is to go to the left or travel west. It would be wise to select a spiritual system that encourages left-handed travel. While it is possible to get to Los Angeles by going right, which is to travel to the east, you will have to go completely around the world to do so. This would require much time and energy that is totally unnecessary. The longer journey, in unfamiliar territory, makes the likelihood of getting lost, injured, or killed along the way much higher. Even Magellan, the first person in history reported to circumnavigate the globe, did not make it all the way home.

We can look at this situation from the perspective of chemistry, as well. Let's say that the result of having a balanced spiritual nature is to have the inner being that is infused with a purple essence. For argument's sake, let's say that the Divine Masculine essence of Peace is colored blue and the Divine Feminine essence of Love is colored red. We know the purple essence is a balance between the red Loving essence and the blue Peaceful essence. But again, that tells us nothing. We cannot move forward or choose a transformation system until we examine ourselves and determine the color of our dominant personal essence. No living being comes to the table of mystical transformation as an empty vessel. Life requires that we have a base energy flowing through our being to be classified as alive. We must examine ourselves

DEMYSTIFYING THE MYSTERY OF MYSTICISM

to find the base energy that flows through our personal spiritual system before we can choose a spiritual path.

So, let's say we do the inner work of self-examination and find that our personal essence is the Loving red essence. What would be required to change the essence in our spiritual system to a balanced state, which is purple? We know from elementary art class that the way to change the color red to the color purple is to add the color blue. We will need to follow a spiritual system that enhances and increases the Masculine essence of Peace, which is blue. This will allow us to achieve an inner being that is balanced and infused with a balanced essence that is purple.

However, what if you found that your inner essence is blue? Would adding more blue essence to your spiritual system get you any closer to reaching the balanced state, which is purple? The answer is: No. Adding more blue essence to a personality that is already infused with blue will just make the inner being bluer. It would cause an already unbalanced system to be even more out of balance than it was before.

This is why randomly doing spiritual practices is not always beneficial and is sometimes dangerous. It is important for you to know and understand *yourself* as well as the destination you wish to reach. The reason is because most spiritual systems operate from one direction or understand the chemistry of spiritual development from the perspective of only one of the two transformational essences. Since there are two divine essences, there are two sets of experiences that lead to transformation: the death of the ego and the birth of the divine male child. Knowledge of the theory is required so that you can choose the path that brings you, the unique individual, to a beneficial result.

19

THE BENEFITS OF MYSTICISM

There are many benefits to becoming a mystic. The first is that you will be able to face life without being run over by it. You will experience calm in most situations because the creative faculties of the mind can be harnessed to solve any problem or overcome any situation. When a stressful event does happen, you are able to quickly rebalance and get back on track. Incidents of illness are reduced and life for the most part is joyful. Once the issues of the past have been processed, we can respond to the outer events of the world instead of reacting from the wounds of the past. Action is taken with an eye to the future. Bringing the best possible outcome that benefits the greatest number of circumstances is the mantra of the mystic. If you get this far in the process of transformation, you will experience a quality of life that the majority of people on this planet only dream of experiencing. Taking control of the body and mind are the life hacks that executive coaches and professional sports trainers teach their clients. Taking control of the body and mind is the secret that turns normal people into extraordinary performers.

The true mystic takes the next step, which is to feel and understand the bioelectrical field of the soul. Balancing and strengthening the spirit's bioelectrical field is the basis for all spiritual and religious texts. We will see that each religion has created a unique method of balancing the energies that has become standardized throughout the centuries. We will also see that finding the right belief system for you is highly dependent upon your predispositions, issues, and perceptions. The most adept practitioners come to realize that there is truth in every spiritual teaching, even when those teachings do not benefit them personally. This is because every spiritual system is working to give the same experience, which is the experience of the expanse of the divine. Once the religions are seen as unique recipes to advanced personal development, the awareness of the richness and beauty of the human experience comes into focus.

Until now, enlightenment has been a random occurrence. In the past, only the lucky few landed in the correct religion that would bring them to a higher state of personal development. We are currently in an age where religious belief causes strife within the individual and between belief systems. By understanding these principles, it will be possible to offer advanced personal development to a wider segment of the population and we will be able to offer this training with or without religious philosophies.

HOW TO USE THIS BOOK

Since the transformational process is interconnected, it does not matter where you choose to begin your transformation. Any work you do will affect all the other facets. For some, understanding must begin with the details and build up to the framework. For others, they need to see the overall picture before they can work down to the details. There is no right or wrong way. This book is designed with the same approach as the mystical scriptures, which means that it can be read from either direction. One of the things that mystics know is that the road to personal transformation runs both ways. The processes of transformation follow a universal order that can be unwrapped from either direction.

Those who are brand new to mysticism will benefit from reading this book from beginning to end. It presents the basics, beginning with the realm of the physical body, moving to the realm of the mind, and ending with the realm of the spirit , which includes the universal framework. Those who are experienced practitioners will benefit from reading this book backwards. The framework of the mystical system, in chapter seven, will give the experienced practitioner an overall picture that will help them understand why they, or their students, run unwitting into roadblocks along the path to personal transformation. The beauty of mysticism is that it is your journey and you are in control of the direction of travel.

THE MYSTICAL MATRIX

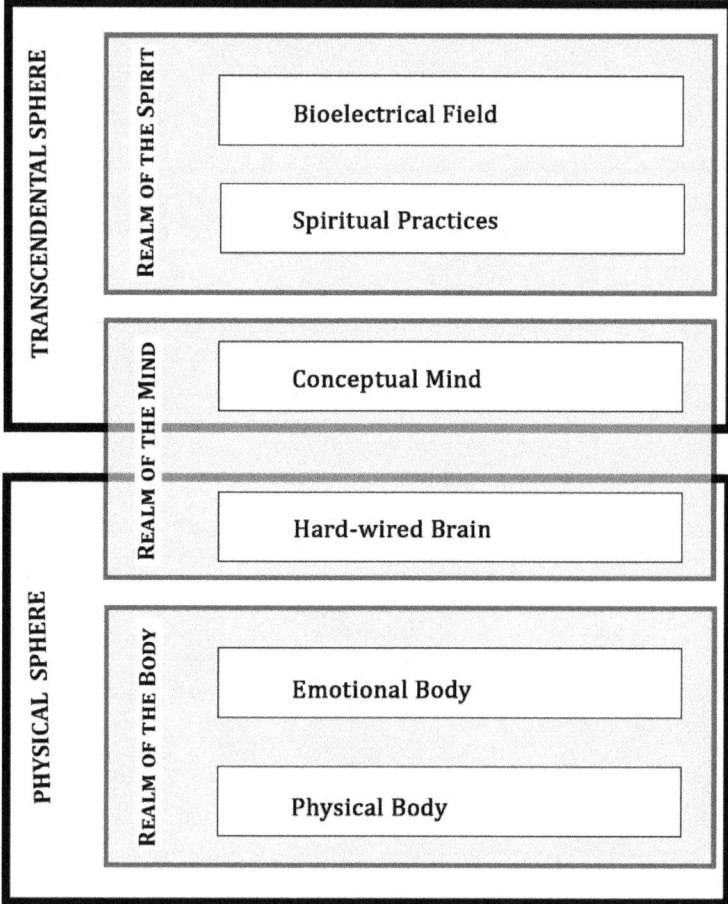

TRANSCENDENTAL SPHERE

REALM OF THE SPIRIT

Bioelectrical Field

Spiritual Practices

REALM OF THE MIND

Conceptual Mind

Hard-wired Brain

PHYSICAL SPHERE

REALM OF THE BODY

Emotional Body

Physical Body

CHAPTER ONE
THE CIRCUITRY OF THE BODY-MIND-SPIRIT COMPLEX

Okay, so you want to be a mystic. It all seems quite wonderful to have experiences of the divine and continuously remain in an altered state of luscious consciousness. Well, I've got news for you. The process of becoming a mystic is called *"The Work"* for good reason. I am not going to lie to you. Under the best of circumstances, becoming a mystic requires all the dedication and persistence you can muster, and more. It is the hardest discipline to master. So, what does it take to achieve these expanded states? What do you need to know? What do you have to do? Before we can answer these questions, we must understand what mysticism truly is.

When we look deeply into the nature of the human creature, we find that there are levels of existence that move from the physical solid form to the most sublime essence. We have a solid body that needs a physical pump to bring nutrients to each cell and we have spiritual essences that are directed by breath and thought. In between the solid and the sublime, we have a conceptual mind that ranges from harboring many fears to allowing us to merge with the oneness of consciousness. The health and harmony of the body, mind, and spirit defines the quality of the human experience.

There are two facets in each realm, the active facet and the passive facet. The active facet is physical or conscious, while the passive facet takes place unconsciously or is the result of processes that have taken place in the active facet. Each layer interacts with the layers below and is associated with multiple realms and spheres. When any facet is activated, it influences the entire realm that it is in, which then influences the sphere that it resides. You will notice that the realm of the mind is the bridge between the spheres. Once the mind is activated, it will spread the influence to the other sphere and then to the furthest realm.

The goal of the mystic is to have full conscious control over all the facets of the body-mind-spirit complex, which includes both the active and the passive facets. It is important to understand that controlling the passive facets requires extensive practice and expanded awareness.

THE BODY

In the body, the pumping of the heart circulates a physical liquid we call blood. This represents the active circulation. This active system is very physical. It involves an organ that physically pumps blood, which is a liquid we can see. The blood actively provides nutrients and takes away waste from every cell in our body. If the heart stops beating, or if we lose too much blood, then the body will die within minutes.

Measurement is the basis of this completely physical realm. We can measure all parts of the body. It is possible to measure sugar levels, cholesterol levels, and even map our DNA. When we discipline the body, we are not talking about some kind of horrible punishment. What we are doing is taking control of the body's physical needs because it will make the body more efficient and healthy. We need a healthy body because it is the base for all further spiritual development. We begin by substituting healthy foods to replace the items that are filled with calories that contain no nutritional value. We add very short exercise routines in the beginning and build over time. We make sure that we are getting the proper amount of rest by enforcing bedtimes and doing relaxation practices throughout the day and before going to sleep.

Emotions are derived from a complicated system of hormonal and chemical cascades. These chemical recipes dictate how we feel when we encounter different situations. The manufacture of hormones and chemicals takes place without a single conscious thought. If we feel threatened, regardless of whether it is our physical body or our personal beliefs, the body will begin the manufacture of chemicals to circumvent that threat, which is known as the fight or flight response. This survival instinct is a built in feature of the human body. We all experience the chemical cascade of fear when we mistake the garden hose for a snake. Our breath quickens and our heart starts racing before we consciously decipher that what we are actually looking at is a harmless garden hose. If it truly were a snake, then the body would be prepared to either kill the snake or get away quickly. Either way, it takes several minutes for the body to return to a calm state because we must clear these chemicals out of the system. Understanding the way the body works is the first step in taking control of the emotions. We will be looking at ways to retrain your emotions and keep them from causing continual torment.

THE MIND

The next realm is the mind. The mind is unique because it is the bridge between the physical and transcendental sphere. Once an activity reaches the realm of the mind, both spheres will be influenced. An event that has triggered the fight or flight response, will cause an emotional cascade within the body and a change in the brain's waves. The change in the hum of the neurons will influence the harmonics of the bioelectrical field because the mind is a bridge and it can operate from both directions. The chemistry of the body will effect the operation of the brain, which then affects the energy field. Or, the energy field of the spirit will set the tone of the brain's waves, which will then affect the physical sphere of the body.

The active facet of the mind is the hard-wired brain. The newest scientific discoveries are showing that the brain is hardwired and does not operate primarily on the right or left side. Researchers have successfully mapped the neural pathways of the brain using functional MRIs. They have found that the brain works in circuits. Currently, there are three main brain circuits: the executive function circuit, the imagination circuit, and the awareness circuit. Most people process incoming information through a favored brain circuit. Logical people have a tendency to stick with the executive function circuit, while emotional people like to cling to the imagination circuit. The awareness circuit gives us the ability to relate outside events to ourselves. It is the circuit of association. The mystic will seek to balance the brain's functioning by exercising the weak pathways so that they can consciously choose how to process an event.

In addition to the specific pathways of the neurons, the hum of the neurons firing creates a frequency that can be detected. Each frequency relates to the type of consciousness the brain is experiencing at the moment. When we train the brain, it is possible to put the mind into specific states, like relaxation or creativity. The third part of the physical brain is the chemistry. Our brains produce chemicals like dopamine, serotonin, and noradrenalin. Interruptions in the manufacture of these chemicals can cause everything from mood disorders to serious diseases like Alzheimer's or Parkinson's disease.

The passive facet of the brain is what I call the "conceptual mind." The conceptual mind is much more than an imagination that dreams up pretty ponies. It is the interpreter of experience. It has a poetic quality that uses imagery and sensation as the backdrop for realization, which is basis for creating meaning to our existence. The conceptual mind can also be trained to solve problems and to strategize for a better future. The well-developed conceptual mind uses all the circuits of the brain simultaneously. It can visualize multiple outcomes and then use logic to select the best solution. However, the conceptual mind can also envision danger when there is nothing to fear. It has a tendency to use past events to judge current situations and it can get stuck in a rut of self-doubt and condemnation. The mystic will take active steps to cleanse the conceptual mind of issues and train it to bring benefit instead of distress.

THE SPIRIT

The final realm of personal development is the spirit. This realm is completely vibrational. It contains both the spiritual practices and the bioelectrical field of the soul. The active facet of the spirit consists of spiritual practices and rituals. The rituals and practices that you choose will affect not just this facet, but all the other facets, as well. Just as a sick body cannot reach the heights of awareness, an unbalanced or stagnant energy field can cause physical illness or mental distress.

Every spiritual practice is designed to enhance, even change, the bioelectrical vibrations of the spirit. When we first do a spiritual practice, it is important to notate how we feel both during and after we have completed it. If the result of a specific practice is not a positive shift in our energy, then it is important to change that practice. There are thousands of practices. The goal is to find the practices that bring beneficial change to our spirit. As we become more adept, just doing a practice is not enough. The aim of the true mystic is to become aware of how the energies are moving within your spiritual system, while you are practicing. Once we are aware of the energy flows, we then learn what practices will adjust our bioelectrical field. Knowing the circumstances when a vibration can heal, or when a vibration can destroy, is the most sublime lesson of the mystic. No one can be considered a master until they are proficient in detecting this sublime truth.

The first spiritual practice that is taught to aspiring students is breathing rhythmically and deeply from the diaphragm. This allows more breath and a greater circulation of energy throughout the spiritual facet. It relaxes the muscles and brings peace to the mind. Many spiritual practices rely upon the breath because the breath is the circulating force, or the pump, of the spiritual energies. The Hindu faith has studied the breath for thousands of years. They have developed an extensive list of breathing exercises and practices. The practices of yoga, tai chi, and qi gong link the exercise of the body to the breath. These practices regulate and exercise both the body and the spirit in one go.

Practices like singing or chanting exercise the breath, the conceptual mind, and the vibrational state of the spirit all at the same time. Singing requires the regulation of the breath, while the words implant conceptual ideas in the mind. When you sing well, you can feel the vibrations reverberate through the body. We know that certain pitches and tones can delight audiences or shatter glass. It is important to choose practices and rituals that will benefit your personality type, your brain's circuitry, and your personal vibrational frequency.

I cannot stress enough the importance of going slowly and modulating your energy system in small increments. Doing extended or intensive practices can cause great harm to the beginning student. Spiritual practice will trigger old wounds and cause distressful events to surface but it should never be the cause of new distress. There is no benefit to blowing a fuse. Blowing a fuse creates a new wound that must be healed, depletes the store of energy that has been accumulated, and forces you to begin again from the point of having no energy.

The passive facet of the spirit is the energy circulating through the body. We find the energy healing systems of reiki, acupuncture, medical qi gong, and prana in this facet. Unlike the dualistic religions that designate one energy as all-good and the other energy as all-bad, the mystic understands that the two energies are interdependent and need to be in balance. Neither is bad or good in and of itself. However, there are negative aspects of both energies when they appear in their unbalanced extremes. The Taoist system of yin and yang incorporates this type of understanding.

The mystic also understands that the dual aspects of good and bad assigned to the two divine energies can be reversed depending upon the culture, belief system, or religion. The Hindu religion considers the Divine Feminine Fire energy to be beneficial and their spiritual rituals honor and work to achieve the rise of the Fire energy. The compassionate practices of the heart and love are the supreme tenants of Hinduism. This exact same energy is symbolized as the serpent and condemned as Satan in the Christian theology. In Buddhism, the teachings are all about putting out the fires of desire with the Divine Masculine Water energies and reaching clarity and a peaceful existence. Which is truth? The answer is:

The Truth is Balance.
The path to balance is different for each person.

Some will need to increase the Fire energy of compassion and Love, while others will need to fill themselves with the Water energy of logic and Peace.

Once you have experienced the spiritual energies flowing through your body, the mystical scriptures of every religion will open for you. Since the mystical scriptures are manuals on how to change and manage the bioelectrical field of the spirit, it is impossible to interpret any of them until you know how the energy flows within yourself. Buddha's flower sermon, Jesus' story of the mustard seed, and the Nativity story are easily understood as three different ways of explaining the same phenomenon once you have experienced the peaceful flow of the Water energy. The rise of the Fire energy, known as Kundalini in the Hindu belief system, is always described as a dynamic event. It is easy to understand why the use of such metaphors like an earthquake, a volcano, a crucifixion, and the rumble of a multitude of horsemen that bring devastation to the current way of life are used to depict this mystical event. Until you have experienced these events for yourself, the mystical texts are just outlandish gobblety gook that seems to come from the mind of a crazed maniac.

The final area of awareness is the expanded consciousness itself. This is the destination of all religion and belief systems. This expanse is unknowable and indescribable. It is the sensation of completely merging into the oneness of all creation. Maslow named this phenomenon, "a peak experience." This is the pinnacle of human capability and most everyone has had a glimpse of this understanding at one time or another. The goal of the mystic is the ability to reach this state at will. What is interesting about the peak experience is that it has been described as both absolute light and complete darkness. We will see why this is so later on.

The Realm
of the
BODY

CHAPTER TWO
THE PHYSICAL BODY

The physical body is the most obvious place to start our transformation. Opening our awareness to how we treat the body is the first step along the mystical path. In many cases, we are unaware of how our actions affect the functioning of the body. We like to eat junk food and be continually excited by activities, or events, that keep us up late and exhausted. While our body has the ability to adapt to many temporary conditions, it cannot function properly with continual abuse. Stress and illness will finally take its toll and cause major medical problems.

Keeping a record of what you eat, how much you exercise, and the amount of rest you get each night is an easy way to become conscious of how you are treating your body. This is your personal journal. It is not for anyone else to see. The only person who will be evaluating what your journal contains is you. It does not matter if you use an old-fashioned notebook and pen or a high-tech app. What matters is that you keep a record, somewhere, some how. The most important aspect of this journal is honesty. If you cannot be honest with yourself, then you do not have what it takes to be a mystic. Coming to grips with who you are, both the good and the bad, is a fundamental part of the journey. Just remember, this is your journey and you have control over what changes and how fast. Don't forget that the three realms of body, mind, and spirit are interwoven. It could be that your cravings are connected to a childhood event. Once that issue is dissolved, that craving will disappear. It might be that cravings for goodies calms down and disappears when you increase the energy within your bioelectrical field. Make notes about these things in your journal as well.

DIET

The chemistry of the body is delicate. So, it is important not to shock the system by making drastic dietary changes. Moving gradually to a diet that is comprised of fresh produce and organic meats is the first goal. It is important to understand that processed foods are full of salt, sugar, and chemical additives, which are quite addictive. It will take an extended amount of time for you to totally eliminate the desire for them. Be gentle with yourself. Add more and more fresh, unprocessed foods to your diet. Consciously substitute healthier alternatives in place of your cravings. When you have a craving for a snack, like a cookie, eat a healthy choice first. If you still crave that cookie after eating the healthy alternative, then you can allow yourself to have that cookie. Since you have eaten a healthy alternative first, you most likely will not be able to eat very many cookies. This stops those cookie jar emptying habits.

Do not automatically assume that every mystic is required to be a vegetarian. There are an unlimited number of dietary programs to choose from. Your body might need a high protein diet to function at its highest potential. Choosing a dietary plan is not about doing what other people do. This about exploring all the options and finding what is best for you and your body.

Checkout the storehouse of knowledge found in the ancient eating systems. The Hindu tradition of Ayurvedic medicine is over 3000 years old and recommends eating according to your body's dosha, or type. This system recognizes that not everyone is exactly the same. Some bodies run hot and process food very quickly, while others run slowly and take a very long time to process food.

Another ancient system of wellness is Traditional Chinese Medicine (TCM). While TCM does heal illness, its first aim is to prevent sickness. TCM looks at all the facets of the person and works to put the physical and energetic systems back in balance. This can be done with diet, exercise, and medicinal herbs. Long-term illnesses, that are caused when the energy system or the physical chemistry of the body is out of balance, respond to the gentle changes that TCM uses to rebalance the system. The main tenant of TCM is to "eat only food," which means to avoid unnatural foods like chemical additives, pesticides, and drugs. Stay away from fad diets. Choose a well-rounded plan that will maximize your well-being. Remember, that you are not looking for temporary weight loss, but for balance and life change.

Fasting is not just a spiritual practice. Science is discovering that the body benefits from a daily twelve hour fast. This allows the body to process all food and clear the digestive tract each day. So, it is wise to eat nothing after dinner until you wake up the next morning. This type of fasting, known as intermittent fasting, causes changes to the chemical make up of the body. Insulin levels drop and human growth hormone levels rise. The body also initiates a cellular waste removal processes that break down and metabolize broken and dysfunctional proteins that have built up. Intermittent fasting can also lower damage done by free radicals and inflammation. Lowered inflammation, lower blood sugar levels, and reduced insulin resistance is especially beneficial for the brain. Fasting also increases levels of brain-derived neurotropic hormones that keep the blues away. It can even change how the genes in your DNA express themselves and possibly increase your lifespan.

Fasting does not have to mean eating nothing. Juice fasts are becoming popular. A juice fast allows the body to get nutrients without the need for excessive processing. It is said that when the body is processing food, it can consume about one third of the energy that is harbored in the food. When we eat foods that need little or no processing, more energy is free to go to other uses, which gives a feeling of wellbeing. Fasting, in any form, is not for everyone. It is just another tool in the toolbox that can be useful for some people.

Drink water. Drink water. Drink water. We lose fluids through the skin, from breathing, and of course, through the excretion of urine and stool. These loses must be replaced every day to maintain the balance of body fluids. Our bodies are composed of about 60% water. Water helps us maintain body temperature, transport nutrients and hormones, as well as create saliva and tears. When muscle cells don't have enough water, they don't function to their highest potential, which is why doctors recommend an increased fluid intake while exercising and during physical activity. Dry skin and wrinkles are another side effect of dehydration. When we drink water, we are giving the body a basic element it needs. When we choose this non-caloric beverage that doesn't affect the body's sugar and cholesterol levels, the body gets what it needs without forcing it to do extra balancing work. So, find ways to add more water to your routine. Add a twist of lemon or lime, but stay away from chemical additives, sugar, and artificial sweeteners.

Going vegetarian has become very popular for reasons ranging from compassion for animals to moving to a healthier lifestyle. Meat proteins are very hard for the body to process. They require a lot of energy to digest and this can lower the life-force for some people. However, the body does need protein. While there are many plant-based proteins to choose from, none is complete. It takes a variety of plant sources to create the right blend of proteins the body needs to be healthy. It is important for vegetarians, especially vegans, to understand the nutritional science that underlies their food choices. Living on mac & cheese, ramen noodles, and cheese pizza does not make for a healthy diet, even though they are all vegetarian choices.

It goes without saying that it is best to eat organic, nutrient rich, foods. However, the cost of these items can make this goal somewhat unattainable. Here is my short list of three items that must be organic for me to consume them. Tea is the number one item that I consider must be organic for me to consume. Tea cannot be washed once it has been harvested because the water will release all the tea from the leaves. If that tea was sprayed with chemicals, you are drinking a brew of pure toxicity. I cannot describe the noticeable change in the way my body felt after just a couple of days of drinking only organic tea.

The second item on the must be organic list is wheat. In the U.S., wheat crops are sprayed with weed killer just before harvest. This allows the grain to become uniformly dry so that the maximum amount of wheat can be harvested with the combines. Again, wheat cannot be washed once it is harvested because it will turn into mush. The process of grinding wheat into flour requires the kernels to be as hard and dry as possible. Here again, the chemicals that were sprayed on the wheat are now fully infiltrated into the flour.

The third item that you need to watch is meat and dairy. In this case, what you are looking for are items where the farmer does not use antibiotics and growth hormones. Growth hormones increase milk production for the farmer but leach into the milk itself. These hormones wreck the body's delicate balances by overloading it with artificial hormones that the body cannot process or eliminate. Studies are showing that the early maturity of girls, lifelong hormonal issues for adult women, and the unbalancing of the masculine hormones in men link back to the artificial hormones in milk products. The use of antibiotics makes milk products doubly bad because science is finding that the extensive use of antibiotics creates super germs that cannot be treated.

Do not think that you have to go this path alone. Do not be afraid to reach out to a nutritional specialist. It does not matter if they follow modern scientific guidelines or ancient wisdom, moving toward a healthier way of eating will open your awareness in many ways. When it comes to diet, making conscious choices and disciplining yourself to eat within certain time frames will help the body function better, which will make you feel better.

EXERCISE

Walking upright is required to designate any species as human. Our bodies need exercise. When our species first appeared on the planet, we walked. We walked to find food. We walked to find habitable lands. We walked to trade and commune with each other. Today, many of us work in offices where we are stuck sitting in chairs for hours on end. Sitting all day stagnates the physical systems and weakens the muscles.

It is not necessary to do a grueling workout everyday, but you will need to be consistent. You will need to make time everyday to exercise. A 15-minute walk around the block, walking up the stairs instead of taking the elevator, or getting up and stretching for 5 minutes every hour is all that is needed in the beginning. Find unique and interesting ways to incorporate exercise into your everyday life. Dance while vacuuming. Consciously twist while putting the dishes in the dishwasher. Do bench presses with the reams of paper as you load them into the supply closet. Notice how a small bit of activity can be rejuvenating. Make sure you write down all the unique ways you find to include exercise, in your journal. It will open your awareness to your physical body and how it moves. Writing down your physical activity also reinforces the good feelings and accomplishments in a way that does not create imbalance elsewhere in your life, like eating sugar or caffeine-laced treats and spending money.

Once you have mastered adding little bits of exercise into your daily routine, it is time to add a full-blown workout plan. You will need to schedule your workout time. It can be on your own or in a gym, but you must be diligent about completing your workouts on a consistent basis. You will want to focus on building flexibility as well as strength. Choose a balanced plan that exercises the entire body. If you choose walking as your style of exercise, add arm swings to exercise your upper body and stretches to release tensions. As the body gets stronger, add longer and more challenging walks.

Here again, do not over do. You want to gently activate the body so that it feels good and will look forward to the next exercise session. The exercise gurus who scream, "No Pain, No Gain," do not understand the interconnectedness of the body and mind. Working out until you become sore creates negative reinforcement and over time will create embedded issues that will be hard to reverse. Pain can lead as easily to quitting as it does to success. If you find that you are constantly pushing yourself past normal limits, this might be an issue in the mind. If you plan to reach the heights of human attainment, it is best to leave pain out of the equation.

REST

Just as our bodies require exercise, they need rest. Getting a good night's rest does so many good things for your body. Sleep affects the quality of life. Getting replenishing sleep at night leads to less daytime fatigue, more stamina, and our overall attention is sharper. We can boost memory retention, consolidate memories, and reorganize thoughts when we sleep well. All these things boost creativity. The centers of the brain that control metabolism also control sleep. When you don't get enough sleep, hormones that drive appetite increase. It could be that kicking the habit to graze throughout the day is simply a matter of getting enough sleep at night. Sleep reduces stress and the inflammation it causes. Inflammation, which is linked to heart disease, diabetes, and arthritis, is reduced when we get the standard eight hours of sleep. Lack of sleep affects reaction time and decision-making. Driving while tired can be as detrimental to your ability to maneuver a vehicle safely as having an alcoholic drink. Exhaustion can also bring on feelings of hopelessness. Depression and anxiety can be curbed with quality sleep because emotions are stabilized during our downtime at night. So, make sleep, both quality and quantity, a priority. Discipline yourself to allow for 7-8 hours of rest every night. One of the best ways to induce sleep is the 4-7-8 breathing cycle. You breathe in for the count of four. Then hold the breath for the count of seven. Then breathe out for the count of eight. It is a simple method that brings sleep in just a few minutes.

Sleep is more than just lying still with your eyes shut for eight hours each night. Sleep takes place in stages that make up ninety-minute cycles. In an average night, your mind will go through multiple stages that form five sleep cycles. A small portion of each cycle is dedicated to REM sleep. REM stands for Rapid Eye Movement, which is the physical characteristic of this sleep stage. It is the lightest form of sleep and is best known for being the time when we dream. REM sleep is vital for the body to function at an optimal level. During REM sleep, the body rejuvenates itself. It is during REM sleep that the immune system repairs itself and the cells regenerate. Lack of REM sleep can cause allergies to flair, intestinal problems like Irritable Bowel Syndrome, hormonal imbalances, and neurotoxicity. What is interesting about REM sleep is that the length of time we spend in REM sleep expands through the night. In the early portion of the night, the duration of REM sleep is short. As the night progresses, the length of time spent in REM sleep lengthens. The longest and most productive session of REM sleep happens in the fifth and final cycle just before you wake up in the morning. When only six hours of sleep a night is allowed, you miss out on the longest session of restorative sleep.

In our stress filled world, sleep can be very illusive. Our daily habits can be just as much a factor in our inability to get rest as staying up half the night playing the latest video game. Consuming caffeinated drinks after 2pm, drinking alcohol late into the night, and watching the late night news or scary movies can wreck havoc with your sleep patterns. Notice how these things are affecting you on a day-to-day basis. Write down your findings and work to change habits where you can.

While stuffing your belly full just before bed will disrupt your sleep, going to bed hungry also negatively affects your quality of rest. If you must eat before bed, choose food items that contain a combination of protein and tryptophan, like yogurt with a little granola added. Tryptophan is an amino acid that converts to the sleep-promoting hormone serotonin.

It is not just the mind that needs to cool down for rest to take place. Our bodies need to physically cool down in order to reach dreamland. Soaking in a hot bath just before bed can actually hinder your ability to fall asleep. So, jump in the tub as soon as you get home from work, instead. This way your body has time to cool down before going to bed.

Another biological influence on sleep is light. It is important to reduce the light in your surroundings just before bed. When you reduce the light in your environment, it signals the body's biological clock to start getting ready for sleep-time. This means turning off the TV, phone, and tablet. The light from these devices tells the brain that it is not time to start producing sleep-inducing serotonin. Note the changes you make to your sleep routine in your journal. Record the difference in how you feel and function when you follow through on your goal of getting sleep that is both restful and rejuvenating.

Rest is more than just sleeping at night. It is important to consciously relax throughout the day. Scheduling a time to relax is just as important as scheduling a time to exercise and sleep. The more consistent you are with taking time to relax, the better you will be in facing the unexpected events that cause stress levels to rise.

There are overwhelming benefits to relaxing. You can reduce muscle tension, relieve chronic pain, reduce anxiety, and feel at ease and in control of your life in general. A number of studies are linking stress with dementia and Alzheimer's disease because stress increases the production of certain proteins in the brain that accelerate the development of these diseases. Stress is also known to produce cortisol, a hormone that increases junk food cravings, lowers serotonin production, and inhibits the manufacture of dopamine in the brain. Relaxation techniques help to reduce stress and in turn reduce the impact of stress on overall health.

Like diet and exercise, relaxation routines need to begin small. Taking a minute to breathe deeply from your diaphragm is the first step. Breathing deeply is not just relaxing, it slows the mind and allows it to reorient away from panic and toward thinking of available options. It cleanses the lungs and oxygenates the blood. It slows down the heart rate and lowers blood pressure. It slows the metabolic rate. It encourages muscles to relax and reduce the tension they are holding. There are thousands of relaxation techniques. Here is just a short list of possibilities:

- Use body-scanning techniques where you consciously relax a single body part, like your neck or shoulders, or your entire body from the head down or from the feet up.
- Sit in nature.
- Take a gentle stroll.
- If you can't sit in nature, listening to nature soundtracks of a bubbling brook, gentle rain, or bird calls for a few minutes a day.
- Listening to binaural wave music.
- Read a book.
- Turn off electronic devices like TV, tablet, and phone for specific periods of time during the day.

Make a point to spend time in nature. When possible, do your relaxations, walks, or exercise in a park or wilderness area. Rent a cabin in the woods or near a lake where there is little access to phones and television. Notice how nature is constantly working but is never stressed. Take time to feel the quiet and soak in the calm. Dare to go barefoot. Feel the earth and your connection to it. This will do more than relax the body and calm the mind. It can start the opening of the spirit to the mystery that surrounds us.

Diet, exercise, and rest are essential practices. But, they are only the beginning of your path towards becoming a true mystic. The next chapter explains the chemistry that is created when the practices of healthy diet, moderate exercise, and rejuvenating rest become a daily part of your life.

Chapter Three
The Chemical or Emotional Body

Underneath every thought, memory, or dream is an ebb and flow of chemicals that dance through the body and brain. The chemistry of the body and brain is responsible for all feeling that we humans experience. The urge that makes you want to run for your life or just sit and relax is a result of a chemical cocktail whipped up by the body and brain. These complex chemical mixtures create our feelings and are like watercolors that permeate our perceptions and memories. There is a big difference in experience when we are under the influence of a mixture of happy chemicals in comparison to when we are under the influence of a collection of negative chemicals. A meeting with our boss can be seen as either a coaching, or as a reprimand. The difference has nothing to do with what the boss said or did. It all comes down to our feelings at the time. It's important to understand those feelings are governed by the chemistry that is flowing through the neurons of the body and brain at the time of the event.

Our brains use a variety of chemicals, known as neurotransmitters, to communicate between nerve cells. As these chemicals surge through the neural pathways, they activate the nerve cells in the body, which relay information from the site of activation to the brain and back again. Neurotransmitters trigger the neurons to fire in sequence up the line, which creates an electrical pulse. There are chemicals that bring excitement and chemicals that calm us down. There are chemicals that detect sugar in the stomach and chemicals that make you aware of a full bladder. The neural system is in a state of constant motion throughout the body. It is electrical energy + motion. You would think that this chemical and electrical system would be nothing more than an automated configuration. However, we humans are much more than a sum of our parts. The electrical system of a house or a car does not give either the ability to feel, but that is exactly what is happening inside the human body.

Researchers are finding that when we change the neural chemistry, we change the experience of life. This is not a new discovery. Ancient peoples were well aware of the affects of hallucinogenic substances. There are many reports of concoctions they brewed up to give a wild ride through the unconscious. But before we jump on the bandwagon of the pharmaceutical industry, lets put the idea into our minds:

It is possible to control the body's chemistry by natural means.

The first step to bringing the emotions into balance is to provide the body with the nutrition, exercise, and rest it needs to produce the variety of chemicals it uses on a regular basis. When the body does not get the basics for producing the positive chemicals it uses, the system will over-load the circuits with stress inducing compounds. When the neural chemistry is out of whack, your feelings will be erratic. Disciplining your body pays off in the long run because making yourself walk each day and denying yourself that sugar-laced donut coupled with that caffeine-loaded concoction could truly bring joy to your life.

Please Note: If you and your doctor decide that an anti-depressant or mood changing drug is the best course of action for your situation, then please feel free to take advantage of modern science's discoveries. You might have a genetic predisposition that requires a lifelong need for synthetic drugs. It could be that you need a prescription for a short time to boost you out of a rut, but then can taper off the usage as the body starts to regulate itself. I'm all for using the tools of modern science when the circumstance dictates, so do not think that you have to go this road without the help of a qualified medical professional and the prescriptions that modern science has formulated.

I will not kid you. It takes great strength to detach from the feelings of the moment. Knowing that what you feel is just a chemical reaction can help, but trust me it is very hard to prevent yourself from running after those things that make you feel better or attacking anything that makes you feel angry or miserable. I, to this day, share the laments of many saints throughout the ages – "I knew better, but I could not do better," and so will you. When you are under the influence of a chemical cascade, it takes superhuman awareness to not repeat your typical cycle of behavior. Notate every reaction in your journal. Question every response, but be gentle with yourself. With vigilance and continued practice, you will be able to pick up on the warning signs earlier and earlier, until one day you have the ability to prevent the chemical cascade from happening in the first place. So, let's examine the very basics of the body's neurological structure.

The cells that make up the brain and the nervous system are called neurons. Unlike other cells in the human body that have a regular shape, these cells have many branches called dendrites. These finger-like branches interlink with the dendrites of the surrounding cells. Each dendrite has receptors that receive chemical and electrical signals from neighboring neurons. The exchange of information takes place in a synapse, which is a tiny gap between the neurons. When a neuron is activated it releases a chemical message into this tiny gap to activate the next neuron in the chain. Like a bucket brigade, the electrical impulses and the chemical signals are sent and received throughout the brain and to the rest of the body. The neurons at the end of the line can trigger muscles to move, stimulate glands into operation, or instigate a new chain of messages. When these processes do not work correctly, your mental state and the ability to physically move your body can be adversely affected.

In many ways, we are cursed by the way our brains are configured. Modern humans are still using an operating system that was developed for primal man, who needed to have a way of dealing with deadly attacks from ferocious animals and other men. In these cases, the brain sends out signals that shut down all unnecessary functions so that all remaining systems can work to fight off the threat or run far away – fast. This system has insured the survival of human kind, but now, the stresses of modern life are triggering those survival responses even though we rarely encounter a life-threatening situation in the midst of our day. Let's look into how this built-in system works so that we can work to circumvent it from causing further misery in our lives.

Below the frontal lobes is the part of the brain that is devoted to survival. These centers govern the basic functions of life. Sleep, hunger, sexual drive, breathing, and heart rate come under the command of the lower regions of the executive function. As long as life is going well, the survival centers send messages of excitement, satisfaction, and joy that pump up your motivation and help you maintain attention. These messages don't interfere with your working memory until there is a logjam of information coupled with a series of minor crises. We can handle the phones that are ringing off the wall when the secretary calls in sick. But, we lose all composure when these distractions are topped off with a failed business deal or a flat tire on the highway. The brain first goes into panic mode and then moves into survival mode. The higher reasoning goes into lockdown, which prevents intuitive learning and nuanced understanding. When the frontal lobes become overloaded, we begin to fear that we can't keep up, or that life is hopeless. Once this happens, the lower regions of the brain take over. The deep regions respond to the overload messages by firing alarm signals of fear, anxiety, anger, or distraction strategies like the need to eat, desire for sex, or depression. Survival signals are overpowering. The entire body responds by shifting its chemistry, respiratory, cardiovascular, and peripheral nervous systems into high alert. All the while, the ability to think drains away.

It is possible to manage the survival signals and reroute them when they start sending up flairs of distress. The first step in managing the lower regions of the brain is to manage the body basics of nutritious diet, moderate exercise, and adequate rest. The brain will naturally panic when it is not getting these basics. If you are filling your body with sugary carbs, then the brain suffers from blood sugar highs and lows. Science is finding that the brain functions best when blood sugar remains stable. Long term disabling diseases like Alzheimer's and dementia are less likely to occur when we discipline our eating in a way that keeps the blood sugar levels from fluctuating wildly.

A sedentary lifestyle will limit the production of the feel good chemicals like dopamine and endorphins as well as the recently discovered compounds, brain derived neurotrophic factor (BDNF) and the nerve growth factor (NGF). The best way to stimulate the production of these brain chemicals is to exercise. Exercise is a good way to reroute the brain's natural survival instincts. While you are at work, get up from your desk and walk. Tackling a couple of flights of stairs can also give you the boost you need to stave off the lower brain's distress signals.

Rest is needed to unclog the circuitry of the brain. If you are not getting enough rest, the brain circuits cannot unburden themselves. The unprocessed material that isn't released continues to build up. It is just like a toilet that has been stuffed with wades of paper. Until the clog is cleared, any additional information just backs up and pours a nasty cocktail of panic inducing chemicals into the other biological systems. So, how do we know that we are getting enough rest? One of the best ways to tell that you are getting enough rest is the ability to sleep through the night and wake up the next morning without an alarm.

Another way to manage panic attacks is to breathe. When the body goes into survival mode, it pumps up the heart rate and quickens the breath. Once we are aware of these changes, we can consciously reverse them by taking deep, smooth rhythmic breaths. Slowing the breath will slow down the heart. Since the heart pumps rhythmically, it makes sense to breathe in a rhythmic pattern. Try breathing in for the count of four and breathing out for the count of six. Since our biological systems work in synchronization, taking conscious control of the breath will affect other parts of the anatomy that we do not generally have control over, like the heart rate.

The second step is to breathe smoothly. Don't pant or gasp. Breathe slowly and smoothly. The heart will then slow, and the brain will open back up so that we can take control of the senses and get the whole system back into a relaxed and confident mode. The rhythm induces the brain into a coherent wave pattern that maximizes the brain's ability to think and solve problems. This is not woo-woo new age spiritual baloney. This is basic physiological science. These are the things that are being taught to Olympic athletes and top executives around the world. The ability to keep calm in a crisis and to calm yourself down after the survival response has been triggered is a skill that takes continual practice. Training the mind to stay focused on remaining in a rhythmic breath pattern will strengthen the executive function circuit. It will keep the higher mind in command of the situation, which gives you the ability to recover from a triggered response quickly.

As you progress, it will take larger and more intense incidents to trigger the survival response. When we look at each firing of the survival response as an opportunity to practice, we again circumvent the survival response. Here is where attitude, which is part of the transcendental side of the mind, has as much to do with successfully managing the survival response as the physical control of the body systems.

There are also many ways that this system can break down. A lack or overload of any one neurotransmitter can cause a number of different illnesses, with depression being the most common. Depression can be a very hard milady to treat because it can be caused by so many diverse factors. Disruption in sleep patterns, eating too much or too little, and lack of energy are other symptoms of a nervous system dysfunction. Brain chemistry is also the basis for addiction. The drive to feel pleasure is regulated by the chemicals in our brains. When our brain chemistry is out of alignment, we tend to crave things like sugar, sex, alcohol, and excitement to bring the brain chemistry back into alignment. The downside of this is that the brain eventually becomes numb to our favorite pick-me-ups and requires more and more of a stimulus to get the same pleasurable effect. The only way to bring the system back to normal functioning is to stop all use of the addictive substance or behavior. This process is very painful and full-blown addiction can be restarted again with just the smallest taste of the addictive substance.

Here is a short list of the neurological chemicals that control the physical and emotional response.

THE NEUROLOGICAL CHEMICALS

GLUTAMATE – is known as the brain's "on switch." Glutamate is the most common neurotransmitter. Whenever this neurotransmitter docks, it causes the neuron to become excited enough to fire. This neurotransmitter is important during early brain development. The electrical impulses that glutamate generates help to create new neural pathways in early childhood. Our bodies can breakdown and process the glutamate that naturally occurs in plants and animal protein. When glutamate is processed into synthetic chemicals, like monosodium glutamate (MSG), the body cannot break it down. The result is a chemical overload that keeps the body in an over excited state.

Deficiency - Problems in creating and circulating glutamate can lead to autism, obsessive-compulsive disorder, schizophrenia, and depression.

Overload - Too much glutamate can cause overexcitement of the neurons, which can lead to cell damage and eventually cell death. High concentrations of glutamate can cause the neural system to become oversensitive, which means that it takes less glutamate to excite a cell.

GAMMA-AMINOBUTYRIC ACID – also known as GABA, this is the brain's off switch. It works to block the surrounding neurons from firing. It is a natural tranquilizer and slows the down the brain and calms nervous activity. Without GABA, the nerve cells fire too often and too easily. Drugs that increase the amount of GABA in the brain have a relaxing, antianxiety, and anti-convulsive effect. It is also used for promoting lean muscle growth, burning fat, and stabilizing blood pressure, and relieving pain. It is thought that GABA cannot cross the blood brain barrier, so taking supplements to increase the levels of GABA in the brain are ineffective. The way to boost GABA in the brain is to boost those things that are needed for the brain to create GABA.

The necessary components for the brain to produce GABA are vitamin B-6 and magnesium. Insuring that the body's B-6 and magnesium levels are normal will naturally bring up the GABA levels in the brain. Tomatoes and valerian root are great ways to boost GABA in your body.

Deficiency - Lack of this neurotransmitter can lead to anxiety, epilepsy, and destruction of the neurons due to overexcitement.

Overload – Too much GABA leads to sleepiness and sluggishness. If you are susceptible to serious depression, do not supplement the amount of GABA because it can trigger a depressive episode.

SEROTONIN – is associated with mood and the overall state of mind. It controls the body clock and is responsible for a good night's sleep. Serotonin also plays a key role in the GI tract by regulating bowel function and movements. When you eat something toxic or irritating, serotonin is released to quickly expel that toxin through diarrhea. Serotonin is made in both the brain and the intestines, but serotonin cannot cross the blood-brain barrier. So, all serotonin that is used for mood enhancement in the brain must be produced in the brain. While it is possible to measure the levels of serotonin in the blood, it is not known if this influences the levels of serotonin in the brain. It is unknown if the dip in serotonin causes depression or if depression causes lower levels of serotonin. There are not any foods that directly increase the levels of serotonin but it is possible to increase the levels of tryptophan, which is a major component in the making of serotonin. Other ways to increase the body's ability to make serotonin, in the brain, is to decrease light before sleep.

Deficiency – Low levels of serotonin can be caused by lowered production by brain cells, a lack of receptors that receive serotonin, inability of the serotonin to reach the receptor sites, and shortages of the tryptophan, a building block of serotonin. Any one of these factors can lead to depression, obsessive-compulsive disorder, anxiety, panic and excessive anger.

Overload – Drugs like Ecstasy and LSD cause a massive release of serotonin. Once the natural stores of serotonin are depleted, users plummet into a depressive state that can only be relieved by another round of massive serotonin release. Cocaine and MDMA prohibit the reabsorption of serotonin once it has been fired in to the synapsis, which is how these two drugs create their highs. A persistent high level of serotonin leads to continuing bowel issues, lowered bone density, excessive blood clotting, and migraines.

ACETYLCHOLINE – The primary function of acetylcholine is stimulation of the muscles, specifically the heart muscles and chest muscles that regulate breathing. It also appears to be important in learning and memory. It plays a critical role in the formation of memories, verbal and logical reasoning, and the ability concentrate. It boosts the theta waves and improves the encoding of new memories. It also encourages the healthy growth of synapses throughout the brain. Researchers are finding that neuroplasticity appears to be dependent upon the presence of acetylcholine. The body can naturally produce acetylcholine from any source of choline. Low fat dairy, eggs, seafood such as salmon, cod, and scrimp, nuts, and oat bran all contain the basic ingredient choline.

Deficiency – There is a link between acetylcholine and Alzheimer's disease. Alzheimer's sufferers have 90% less acetylcholine in their brains than people whose memory functions normally. Lack of this neurotransmitter can also cause Myasthenia Gravis, which is characterized by weak muscles and fatigue. Treatments for Myasthenia Gravis inhibit the production of the balancing neurotransmitter, acetyltransferase, so that the acetylcholine has more time to interact with its receptors before being deactivated in the synapse.

Overload – The body has mechanisms to prevent an overload of this neurotransmitter. Excess acetylcholine is usually caused by neurotoxins that inhibit the production of acetyltransferase. The result is that the muscles needed for breathing and pumping the heart are paralyzed. If the overload is not addressed quickly, death is the result.

DOPAMINE – controls movement and the ability to experience pleasure and regulate pain. It enables us to take action and move toward the rewards we see. It releases energy when a great opportunity presents itself. Dopamine plays a role in selecting which action to take. Higher levels of dopamine activity lead to higher levels of motor activity and impulsive behavior. Risk-takers fall into this category. A lack of dopamine can make the pleasure center of the brain inoperative, which leads to lethargy and slowed reactions. Life becomes physically painful and lacking any pleasure.

While dopamine can be found in many foods, it is incapable of crossing the blood brain barrier. It must be created inside the brain to perform any kind of neural activity. Dopamine is also the precursor to other neurotransmitters like norepinephrine and epinephrine. In order to increase dopamine production, look to increase your intake of the building blocks of dopamine. Dopamine is made from the amino acid, tyrosine. Foods high in tyrosine are meat, dairy, oatmeal, eggs, dark chocolate, bananas, green tea, and seaweed. We need a stable source of dopamine, not just for itself, but also so the body can make other neurotransmitters the body and brain uses.

Dopamine acts as a "teaching signal." When an action is followed by an increase in dopamine activity, it is like getting a treat after performing a trick. This built-in system of reward is a form of operant conditioning. In other words, our brains train us. They incite desires and entice us to seek out pleasurable substances and experiences. Most types of reward increase the level of dopamine in the brain. Every addictive substance or pleasurable activity affects the release of dopamine. Dopamine is released in an area of the brain that has been named, "the reward pathway." This circuit connects experience with feeling good. Addiction can be your body attempting to fix an existing problem of low dopamine levels. Setting and accomplishing small goals can boost your dopamine levels without the regret of addictive behavior. A rewarding life is the best defense against addiction.

Do not think that deactivating this built-in reward system will fix the dilemma of addiction. When the reward pathway is rendered inactive in test animals, they do not seek anything, including food, and will starve to death, even if food is placed next to them. Your goal is to learn to harness your reward system in a way that creates a healthy stream of natural dopamine. It will help you feel more alive, focused, productive, and motivated.

The second pathway, known as the nigrostriatal pathway, regulates the motor functions. It is thought that the oxidation of dopamine destroys this pathway and leads to the onset of Parkinson's disease. In this case, exercise is the best thing you can do for your brain. Studies show that exercise promotes the growth of new brain cell receptors and produces not just dopamine but also endorphins. You do not have to complete an exhausting workout to increase your capacity to feel good. No-impact practices like taking a simple walk, yoga, tai chi, or qi gong provide powerful body-mind-spirit benefits.

Deficiency – People with low dopamine activity lack a zest for life and often rely on caffeine, sugar, or other stimulants to get through the day. This group may be more prone to addiction and suffer from lack of motivation, fatigue, mood swings, and memory loss. Parkinson's disease is a direct result of low dopamine. Restless leg syndrome and ADHD are also associated with decreased dopamine levels.

Overload – When dopamine levels are too high, the normally good feelings can turn sour. Agitation, anxiety, stress, hypersexuality, hyperactivity, insomnia, paranoia, aggression, hallucinations, suspicious thinking and mania can be the result of too much dopamine.

ADRENALIN, NORADRENALIN, ALSO CALLED NOREPINEPHRINE – is part of a two-pronged punch of chemicals related to the "fight or flight" response. Norepinephrine is both a hormone and a neurotransmitter. The primary function of norepinephrine is to mobilize the brain, as well as the body, for immediate action. It is the main neurotransmitter used by the sympathetic nervous system. Norepinephrine is responsible for setting your energy levels. While it is released throughout the day and night, the quantity and intensity of release increases in times of stress or danger. It increases arousal and alertness, promotes vigilance, and focuses attention. We want our norepinephrine production to be on point. Not too much. Not too little. When this neurotransmitter is out of balance, our feelings of being energetic and alive can turn into adrenal fatigue.

Norepinephrine affects the sympathetic nervous system by increasing heart rate and blood pressure, triggering the release of glucose, increasing the blood flow to the muscles, and reducing the blood flow to the gastrointestinal system. It is important to note that norepinephrine is synthesized through a series of steps. The body makes its norepinephrine supply by converting dopamine into norepinephrine. When the stores of dopamine are depleted then the body cannot make norepinephrine, which means you will feel exhausted, drained, and depressed.

Deficiency – Lack of this neurotransmitter can lead to critically low blood pressure, making it impossible for a person to stand for more than a few seconds without fainting. When conditions exist that limit the amount of dopamine produced, then the levels of norepinephrine will also be negatively affected.

Overload – Restlessness, stress and anxiety are side effects of a system that is overloaded with norepinephrine. If too much norepinephrine is released over long periods of time it can lead to any number of stress related illnesses, which include glaucoma, migraines, hypoglycemia, multiple effects within the immune system, retention of sodium in the blood stream, and a range of cardiovascular issues.

Cortisol – is the second substance in the "fight or flight" response. It is also known as "the stress hormone." It is different from adrenaline because it takes minutes for cortisol to shift the body into "war alert" and prepare for fighting or running. Cortisol performs many functions. It counteracts insulin and allows sugar to flood into the blood stream. Cortisol is part the cocktail of chemicals that regulate the human sleep-wake cycles, so if your body is on "high alert" it will be next to impossible to get a good night's rest. Cortisol is a diuretic. It increases the amount of water the body excretes. While vital for getting the body moving in times of danger, it is also important that cortisol levels return to normal after a stressful event. In our current high-stress culture, the body does not always have the time to return to normal before the next stressful event takes place.

Cortisol needs potassium in order to operate. When cortisol is put into action, it transports potassium out of cells and replaces it with sodium. When potassium levels are low, cortisol levels decline. When cortisol levels are low, it allows allergens and inflammation to run rampant through the body. Those with rheumatoid arthritis, an inflammatory disease, are known to have low potassium levels.

Cortisol and the stress response is known to have negative effects on the immune system. When cortisol levels are high, it suppresses the immune system and lengthens the time it takes for a wound to heal. Here, again, is a chemical that needs to be in balance so that it can be high enough to control allergens and inflammation but low enough to allow the immune system to heal wounds and fight infection.

Cortisol is not just a hormone that works in the body. It also works with epinephrine in the brain to create flash bulb memories, which are memories of short-term emotional events. However, long-term exposure to cortisol damages cells in the memory centers of the brain, causing impaired learning and memory retrieval.

Ways to reduce cortisol levels in the body include: magnesium supplements, Omega-3 fatty acids, eliminate trans-fats and limit saturated fats in the diet, boost consumption of whole plant foods to maximize the intake of fiber and antioxidants in the diet, ashwagandha root, music therapy, massage therapy, laughing, regular dancing, and daily exercise.

Behaviors that increase cortisol levels in the body are: ingesting caffeine, sleep deprivation, prolonged aerobic exercise, and fasting. Severe trauma or stressful events will also contribute to raising cortisol levels.

Deficiency – Low levels of cortisol causes blood sugar imbalances, such as hypoglycemia, disruption in sleep patterns, fatigue, brain fog, and mild depression. Since cortisol combats inflammation, those who have lower levels of cortisol will experience high levels of inflammation, like arthritis, and suffer from extreme allergies.

Overload – High levels of cortisol can contribute to diabetes, lowered bone density, dampened thyroid function, impair cognitive performance, lower immune function, and increase abdominal fat.

ENDORPHINS – The body produces at least 20 different kinds of endorphins. Endorphins produce calming effects throughout the body and offer pain relief as well as reduction in anxiety. They are naturally produced opioids. They are found in the emotionally charged limbic regions of the brain and are responsible for blocking pain and controlling emotion.

This classification of drug produces the feeling of euphoria. It is widely believed that these feelings of pleasure exist to signal when we have had enough of a good thing, which leads to the feeling of satisfaction. A person who does not have enough endorphins circulating in their brains may never receive the mental signal to stop a behavior, like eating or washing their hands, and will continue until that signal is received. Endorphins may be the cause of the "placebo effect" because they trick the hypothalamus into a sense of well-being.

Naturally produced endorphins are not addictive because once they are released they are immediately broken down by enzymes and recycled for future use. Synthetically produced opiates lock into the same receptors but are not broken down by the body's enzymes. The feelings of euphoria are intensified and extend over longer periods of time. The likelihood of drug dependence increases every time such drugs are used, which is why morphine and heroin are controlled substances.

The primary triggers that release endorphins are based around stress and pain. Vigorous exercise stimulates vigorous breathing, which then stimulates endorphin production and leads to an effect known as runners high. Laughter is another way to stimulate endorphin production. Hot chili peppers, dark chocolate, controlled-breathing exercises, singing, acupuncture, massage therapy, sex, meditation, and even ultraviolet light are other ways to stimulate the release of endorphins.

Deficiency – Low levels of endorphin production may be responsible for obsessive-compulsive disorder. Some people who engage in self-hurting behaviors may do so in part to experience the feeling of euphoria. Lack of endorphins can lead to depersonalization disorder. Abuse, particularly emotional abuse in childhood, natural disasters, war, excessive stress, panic attacks, and cannabis can lead to a depletion of endorphins. Problems with endorphin production may be the cause of clinical depression or sudden shifts in emotions.

Overload – Heightened endorphin levels can cause intensified states of rage or anxiety. It can also cause the hypothalamus to flood the body with "fight-or-flight" signals and instigate panic throughout the body.

CONCLUSION

As you can see, the chemistry of our brain and nervous system is quite delicate. All of these chemicals seek to find a "sweet spot" that represents balance within a complex and interconnected system. Slight imbalances can cause mood swings, muscle impairment, or damage to the brain or nervous system itself. The greatest imbalances come when our bodies are invaded by synthetically produced neurotoxins. A neurotoxin is a chemical that either blocks the natural release of a neurotransmitter or removes all blocks and allows a neurotransmitter to indiscriminately flood the system. Even small amounts can affect the way your mind and body functions.

Pesticides are neurotoxins. Pesticides can be found on the country farm and the city yard. Eliminating foods that contain pesticides, preservatives, and artificial sweeteners can be half the battle of controlling your emotional system. The other half of controlling your emotional system is to control your attitudes and perceptions, which will be covered in chapter five when we discuss the conceptual mind.

The Realm
of the
MIND

Chapter Four
The Hard-Wired Brain

Training the mind is the next phase of mystical advancement. The mind is a unique realm because it straddles the line between the physical and the transcendental spheres. On the one hand, the brain is hardwired with neural pathways that hum at different frequencies. On the other hand, the mind is comprised of thoughts and perceptions that influence our beliefs. You will see that the mind needs the same amount of discipline as the body, maybe even more. In this chapter, we will discuss the training of the physical functioning of the brain. In the next chapter, we will be training our attitudes and perceptions.

The health of the brain's neural pathways is reliant upon the general health of the body. Moving toward a healthy lifestyle is important because it will allow the brain to operate at its highest potential. It is not just diet, exercise, and rest that affect the physical brain. Every time we think, we are strengthening a particular pathway. Just as it is comfortable to travel a familiar road, we generally like to take the same neural pathway when we think. This is not always what is best in every situation we face. Having a wide, creative view is not going to be beneficial in a crisis because a crisis requires a sharp focus that overrides emotions in order to navigate the situation. The same is true for the narrowed one-track mind. Opening the imagination to a variety of possibilities allows creativity to blossom. Understanding what it is like to walk in another's shoes gives us warmth and compassion in our decision-making. It is important that we train all the pathways of the brain so that we can respond in appropriate ways.

Training the mind can be very intense. In many cases, we have plowed deep ruts into the circuitry of the brain. This makes it very hard to change the way we process incoming information. Science is finding that only thirty percent of our brain wiring comes from our DNA. The other seventy percent comes from our experiences in life. Experience causes the activation of neurons. Multiple activations can lead to a change in the connections among neurons, which is the basis for neural plasticity.

From the very first days of life, we embed experience into memory. An experience will include perceptual, emotional, and behavioral neural responses. All of which are embedded into the implicit memory. This is a natural consequence of the brain. Implicit memory records the feelings and perceptions. It is like a piece of watercolor paper. It absorbs and spreads the paint as it is brushed across the paper's fibers. It is very hard to bring these types of memories into consciousness because they are so interwoven into the background of the mind. It is like trying to pick a single color out of a watercolor landscape. Conscious attention is not required for implicit memory to be encoded. It is as if the moments of our lives are silently recorded and imbedded into our minds. Feelings and emotions cannot be expressed as words. These memories do not activate the conscious centers of the brain when they are embedded. We do not have the internal sensation that something is being recorded when an event is placed in implicit memory. The same is true when an implicit memory is accessed. We find that perceptual, emotional, and behavioral response happens without our knowing that we are reacting to something that we have previously experienced. This is something to remember when we look into the unconscious part of the mind and again later when we get to the spiritual realm.

Explicit memory is when we consciously imbed information into our brains. When we study any subject with the intention of being able to recall the information, we are training explicit memory. This type of training will literally burn new pathways into your brain, which is why this type of training can be very hard and mentally exhausting. However, once the information is implanted, recall is easy. In this case, when we are trying to recall the information, it seems as if we are digging through file cabinets or closets to find the information that we consciously stored. It is easy to retrain these types of memories because it is possible to change anything that was consciously stored.

THE CIRCUITRY OF THE BRAIN

Neuroscience is blossoming with new information every day. As the mapping and study of the brain continues, we are seeing new ways to retrain our brains. The experimental lab is putting the ancient ways of the spiritual master to the test. Scientists are watching the brains of master meditators and yogis while they perform spiritual practices. Surprisingly, these advanced practitioners are wowing science with their abilities. Scientists are finding that the master meditators and yogis are able to consciously activate areas of the brain that the average person can rarely access. Researchers are also beginning to see, in real time, how different practices activate different circuits of the brain. Master meditators are showing us that it is possible to take control of our brains and manipulate the way it functions.

This brings us to one of the most amazing facts about our brains. No longer is it believed that we are stuck with a machine that has irreplaceable parts. In a machine, once a part is broken, it will no longer function until it gets a new part. Researchers are finding that our brains are capable of dynamic rewiring, which is known as neural plasticity. Science is showing us that the brain can create new neural pathways and reroute around damaged areas of the brain. When a circuit is damaged or cut off, the brain has the ability to rewire itself. Stroke victims can relearn to walk and talk because the brain can reroute the information and regain its abilities. Science is now experimenting with magnetic stimulation to entice the neurons into healthy synchronous wave patterns. Magnetic stimulation seems to strengthen weak circuits and even grow new neural pathways. Unlike drugs that just medicate the problem, magnetic stimulation seems to physically solve the problems of disconnection by growing new pathways.

With the invention of functional MRI, scientists are now able to study the brain while it is processing the electrical data that comes in from the senses. The old ideas of right-brained and left-brained people have been abandoned to make way for the newest theories of brain function. Currently, science has mapped three brain circuits: Executive Function Circuit, Imagination Circuit, and the Awareness Circuit. Let's look into how each of these circuits influence the way we process information.

THE EXECUTIVE FUNCTION CIRCUIT

The executive function is found in the frontal and prefrontal lobes of the brain. There are two levels in this part of the brain, the higher mind and the survival mode, which we discussed in the previous chapter. The higher level of the executive function is responsible for reasoning, decision-making, organizing information, prioritizing ideas, and time management. It is responsible for juggling the multiple tasks of everyday life. This is the logic center of the brain. Information processed through this pathway is perceived from a linear perspective.

When the executive function is weak, the lower regions of the brain have many opportunities to take over. Survival desires like hunger, sex, and panic have the ability to override all logic and become the driving force in life. This can create so much unnecessary drama and misery in life. When the executive function is properly trained, it is possible to leave that cookie in the jar, make responsible decisions, use time wisely, and bypass stress because your higher mind is able to stay in control.

THE IMAGINATION CIRCUIT

The imagination circuit processes information from a creative or emotional standpoint. When you are remembering a past event, thinking about the future, or imagining alternative scenarios, you are activating the imagination network. It readies us in the present moment to deal with what will happen at a later date. We also use this circuit when we are trying to imagine what someone else is thinking. It is the circuit of daydreams and creative musing. This part of the brain is active at all times. When we are doing mundane things like taking a shower or sweeping the floor, the imagination circuit is busy making connections and imagining different scenarios. It is not until an "ah-ha" moment occurs that the solution, which is the result of much work, emerges into to consciousness.

The imagination is famous for involving many different brain functions like emotions, memory, as well as thoughts and logic. Since the imagination uses so many different brain functions, it requires a home where multiple circuits cross paths. The neocortex and the thalamus control the brain's imagination, along with other brain functions such as consciousness and abstract thought. Having a central convergence point allows a person to make giant leaps of understanding. It also gives the ability to mentally assemble, blend, or disassemble component parts of designs or inventions.

The ability to use the mind to visualize the complete architectural plan of a building was the highly valued skill of the ancient Egyptian architect. Imhotep was the most famous of the Egyptian architects, whose skill was so great that he was elevated to godlike status and was worshipped for hundreds of years after his death. It is important to understand that architectural plans are a relatively recent human accomplishment. The painter-architect Raphael is credited with the invention of the modern architectural plan in the 1500's. Before then, architectural plans were imagined in the mind. Only those who could mentally imagine the design of a complete building or structure would be elevated to the esteemed rank of architect.

Creativity requires that we be open to as many inputs as possible. When we limit our thoughts to the straight and narrow, we close down our ability to make the random connections required for creative thinking. Using the same pathway over and over makes the connections more efficient, but creates ruts in the brain's circuitry. As the connections between neurons become more efficient, your brain starts to behave like a packhorse that travels the same route, day in and day out. Plodding along a beaten path of boring sameness. So, the best way to get the imagination to fire up is to seek out new environments, new skills, or new information where you have no experience. A new experience is a very effective way to unleash the imagination because it forces the brain out of its linear rut.

Creativity is not just about assimilating multiple inputs. It also runs in two directions. While both the mental processing of a video and the mental processing of a daydream run along the imagination circuit, scientific findings are showing that the direction of the path through the brain for each of these phenomena is different. When we watch a video, the eyes channel the flow of information to the visual cortex first and then up to the parietal lobe or thinking center. In essence, *the pictures create thoughts*. However, when we imagine or dream, the information begins in the brain's thinking center and then is moved to the visual cortex. When the process runs in this direction, *the thoughts create pictures*. We will see the importance of this finding when we are training the perceptions and again when we interpret dreams.

The fact that the imagination functions in two directions leads to the two ways of honing the imagination: problem solving and strategy. Strategy involves thinking ahead, to imagine the possible roadblocks in advance and plan for those possibilities. Let's use our imagination to visualize a party with one hundred guests. Now, let's say you would like for your guests to sample an array of goodies in the least amount of time. We use our imaginations to simulate the event before it happens. We watch, in the mind's eye, as our imaginary guests select goodies from our different table layouts. The first table layout consists of the tables placed in a corner up against the wall. We immediately nix this set-up because the access for the guests is limited and the guests will most likely bump into each other in order to get the goodies that are laid out for them. The awkwardness of such a set-up would put a damper on the pleasure of our guests. We then think back to a time when we experienced a truly enjoyable event where the tables were in a straight line and pulled away from a wall. The plates were placed on one end and silverware and napkins at the other. The guests had the ability to access the goodies from either side, in a natural flow. There were now two lines instead of one. If you set up another set of tables in this manner that would increase the number of food lines to four and double the speed at which everyone can be served. Einstein called this type of thinking mind experiments. He used his imagination to simulate experiments in his head. That is how the famous formula of $E=MC^2$ came into being.

On the other hand, problem solving requires the imagination to think backwards, to imagine how the problem arose. You begin with the current situation and must determine how the problem occurred. In most cases, problem solving takes place after an error has happened. So, lets go back to that party with one hundred guests. In this scenario, you did not think ahead and laid out all the snacks on a table in a back corner of the room. As the guests are having trouble navigating the snack area, you realize that this is causing the party atmosphere to turn sour. So, now you have to figure out why there is a problem. You then realize that access to the food is limited because one side of the table is shoved up against the wall and that the curve around the corner is causing confusion as to where to begin. You decide to move the guests away from the area and pull the tables away from the wall so that it will be easier for your guests to select the goodies without mishap. The reverse engineering process uses the same imagination circuit, but in the reverse direction, to find a solution once something goes wrong.

The imagination can also cause great distress when it uses its ability to imagine outcomes in ways that panic our emotions. We can imagine danger to ourselves and loved ones and we can be afraid of things that do not exist. People with vivid imaginations can torment themselves with crippling fears when they have not disciplined their creative mind. Disciplining the imagination to use its gifts for beneficial purposes is the key to a happy and joyful life.

THE AWARENESS CIRCUIT

The awareness circuit processes information from a spatial awareness of the internal and external environment. Awareness requires a triangle of brain functioning. This circuit is a conglomeration of smaller triangular connections that tie three portions of the brain together in a triangular pattern. It looks like a flower that has triangular flower petals encircling the centralized brain structure, known as the thalamus. These petals connect neighboring brain areas to each other. The connections are dedicated to attention processing in the brain.

Awareness involves the operation of attention and how it relates to one's self. To see a lion walking across the savannah is one thing, but additional areas of the brain are required to understand that a lion, coming your way, is not going to be a friendly greeting. We can watch an event, but it does not become true awareness until we see our role in what is happening. The awareness circuit appears to function as an enhancement mechanism within the brain's activity. It is only when we understand the significance of the event in relation to ourselves that the awareness circuit opens. We are not considered aware when we look at photographs of all the litter in the ocean until it dawns on us that our actions have contributed to this environmental tragedy.

The location factor used by the awareness circuit, in many cases, is the physical body. The location of the body in regard to a changing environment, such as a rainy day, will activate the awareness circuit. In this case, the perception is associated with my body experiencing a particular sensation, such as being wet, when we think of a rainy day event. Another way to connect an event with one's self is to link an event to our personal history. Your memories, like the time when a relative passed away or when you experienced an amazing sunrise, can serve as the self-relating event. When we can link an event, a story, or a symbol to a personal memory, it can open the awareness circuit. Opening this brain circuit is key to processing our past because it relates the buried memories to current events, which helps to bring them up into conscious awareness. When this circuit is functioning properly we can understand why certain events cause emotional reactions. Once the memories are out in the open, we can process them and find ways of dealing with those issues.

The event of awareness requires that the attention be directed to the regions of the brain where the self is expressed at the same time that attention is directed to the object. This is an important fact. It is the circuit of association. So, this circuit is not just about selfish or egoistic pursuits. When properly trained, this circuit gives us the ability to walk in someone else's shoes. It gives the ability to see from a perspective that is different than our own, which is the basis for compassion.

It is also the circuit of superstition. Associating an environmental event like an earthquake, or erupting volcano, to my personal wrongdoing is a negative way this circuit is used. The awareness circuit is also the cause of many of our misperceptions. It associates the actions of others to ourselves. Let's say you notice that your neighbor is sitting in his car in the driveway. Most likely they are not sitting there specifically to spy on you. It may be that your neighbor just wanted to finish listening to an inning of an exciting baseball game that is playing on their car radio.

An experience becomes my experience only when the awareness circuit is activated. Here is the key to experiencing the divine.

Until we can relate a symbol, a story,
or a feeling of the divine to ourselves,
we will not have the personal experience
required for transformation to take place.

It is only when the attention includes both the self and an object or event that the term awareness can be given. There can be attention without awareness but awareness cannot happen without attention.

BRAIN WAVES

Our brains hum with the electrical pulses of the neurons as they communicate with each other. This is the root of all our thoughts and behaviors. The combination of millions of neurons sending signals at the same time creates waves that can be detected. The frequency determines the size and shape of the wave, which is also known as bandwidth. Each bandwidth represents a different functionality of the brain. These waves behave like a symphony because all the bandwidths are detectable at all times, but not in the same strengths or volumes. When a slow wave pattern is dominant, we will feel tired or dreamy. When a higher frequency wave is dominant, we will feel alert, excited, or even panicked. Brainwaves can be complex because they produce different effects when they occur in different locations in the brain.

There are five brainwave frequencies that are common to all humans. Men, women, and children of all ages experience the same types of brainwaves. They are consistent across cultures and around the world. Our daily experience of the world is inseparable from our brainwave profile. No matter the frequency, the best brainwaves are the ones that are evenly spaced and alike in size. They should look like continuous flowing loops and not the jagged scribbles of seismic activity. When our brainwaves are out of balance, there will be corresponding problems in our psychological or physical health. Over-arousal in certain brain areas can cause anxiety, impulsive behavior, chronic nerve pain, and sleep disorders. Under-arousal in certain brain areas leads to many types of depression and attention deficit. Things like obsessive-compulsive disorder, bipolar disorder, rage, and panic attacks can be caused by instabilities in the brain rhythms. Knowing how to manipulate the frequency of your brainwaves will allow you to be mentally productive across a wide range of activities. With practice, you will be able to control your brainwaves and set your mind up for a particular activity like sleep, intense concentration, or creative musing.

From ancient times to the present, changing brainwaves involved taking hallucinogenic drugs or medications. While this method does work, it can have negative side effects, like sexual dysfunction. The other way to change your brainwaves is through brainwave training. Getting into a mood of relaxation or contemplation can be as simple as using brainwave entrainment methods such as listening to music, nature sounds, or chiming bowls that include an underlying binaural beat. Knowledge of brainwave characteristics enhances a person's ability to make use of the specialized qualities that each frequency offers.

It is important to know that our brains like to synchronize with other people or with the environment. Have you noticed that when you are around a calm group of people that you feel more at ease? The same is true when you attend a football game. It is utterly impossible for the average person to reach a state of Zen while sitting in the stands. So, it is very important that the people we hang out with are people who are compatible with who we want to be. Spending time with people who thrive on conflict will bring upset and misery to your life.

The environment also affects animals. When the neighbor's dog is yapping, I turn on a soothing sound track of chimes and the dog calms down and eventually stops barking. Screaming hysterically at the dog, or a child, to force them to calm down does not work. When you are in an agitated state, that agitation flows to others around you, like ripples on a pond. So, you must radiate calmness to calm down the child or barking dog.

Let's take a brief look at the different frequencies and how they function in the brain.

DELTA - Frequency range from .1-4 pulses per second.

Delta is the state of unconsciousness or deep sleep. It also regulates the bodily processes such as heartbeat, kidney functioning, and digestive functioning. This state stimulates healing and regeneration, which is why deep sleep is so important to the healing process. When the mind is in the delta wavelength, the body generates chemicals that are depleted while you are awake. The anti-aging hormone DHEA and melatonin are produced only when the mind is functioning primarily in the delta range. Delta waves seem to suppress cortisol, which is a hormone associated with stress. The relaxing effect of delta brainwaves not only put you into a state of deep rest but also can reduce muscle tension headaches and calm anxiety. These waves are slow and very loud. They are deeply penetrating, like a drumbeat.

Extensively experienced meditators can experience the delta state while they are in very deep transcendental meditation when awareness is fully detached. This is the state of full absorption into the void. The delta state is said to be the gateway to the collective unconscious. In this state, we can receive information that is unavailable when we are consciously awake.

THETA - Frequency range from 4-7 pulses per second.

Theta is the twilight state that is experienced when you are falling asleep and just before coming to full consciousness. It is a semi-conscious state that is critical to incorporating long-term memory, especially during REM sleep. This is also where your deepest mental programs are harbored. This wavelength is characterized by pure silence. So, the only way to engage this wavelength is through vivid visualizations. Skilled access to this state gives the practitioner inspiration, exceptional understanding of processes, and insightful creativity. Experienced meditators claim that this is the state of feeling a deep unity with the spiritual universe.

When in the theta state, internal censorship and guilt are turned off so there is a tendency for ideas to flow freely. It can happen while doing any mundane task like taking a shower or vacuuming the rug. When we consciously allow our minds to stay in the theta state for an extended period of time, this allows us to have a free flow of ideas about yesterday's events or to contemplate the activities of the forthcoming day. This time can be extremely productive and can be a period of very meaningful and creative activity.

On the negative side, it is where we hold our fears, troubled history, and nightmares. When we spend time in the theta state, we will run into these issues and fears. It is important to understand this when we are learning to meditate because we can reach the theta state through deep meditation. There are many people who quit meditation because they cannot sit with the fears that are harbored in their own minds. The fact that we are in a state to consciously experience these negative emotions, which are usually buried below the conscious thought process, is the beginning of releasing them as issues from our psyche. This can be a scary and painful process. Only those who can face these negative emotions and past events, as they are presented, will progress into the highest realms of mysticism.

The border between the Theta and Alpha state, located in the ranges between 7 Hz to 8 Hz, is the optimum wavelength for programming and re-programming the unconscious mind. In this narrow section of the spectrum between deep relaxation and conscious awareness, you have the ability to create your reality.

ALPHA - Frequency range is 8-13 pulses per second

This is the state of physical and mental relaxation. This resting state is calm but alert. Since it lies just below the active awareness, it is the first gateway into the subconscious mind. Alpha is the whisper of your intuition, which becomes clearer the closer you get to the lower end of the spectrum. It is the ideal state for creativity. Daydreams, reflection, and general meditation belong to this category. It is the ideal frequency to learn new information, perform elaborate tasks, and analyze complex situations. The attentive relaxation of the mind increases the levels of norepinephrine and dopamine, which is linked to feelings of clarity that can last for hours and even days.

BETA - Frequencies range from 13-38 pulses per second.

This is the normal waking state when our attention is directed towards problem solving, judgment, or decision-making. Beta waves are characteristic of a strongly engrossed mind. This is the brass in the orchestra. You can't miss it. In the lower frequencies, it can feel as if life is efficient and well structured. We are able to handle much of what is happening and are enjoying the activity that this frequency can bring.

Beta, when it is associated with upper frequencies in the range, corresponds to feeling agitated, stressed, and afraid. We can experience the beta wavelength as the badgering inner critic that gets louder and louder as the pulses get faster and faster. It seems that the faster this wave goes, the more negative consequences appear. Continual high frequency processing is very inefficient. It takes tremendous amounts of energy to keep going at this pace. When we force the brain to process that this level for long periods of time, it causes mental fatigue and exhaustion, which can create an unending loop of negativity and hopelessness.

GAMMA – Frequencies range from 38-60 pulses per second

Gamma waves are the fastest brainwaves. It is also the subtlest brainwave and it occurs when simultaneous processing of information from different areas of the brain takes place. It passes information rapidly and can only be accessed when the mind is quiet. The high pitch of gamma waves can be related to the flute in an orchestra. A flute cannot be heard when the brass horns of the beta waves overpowers it. Since gamma is above the frequency of neuronal firing, how it is generated remains a mystery. Researchers have discovered that gamma waves are highly active when an experienced meditator is in a state of universal love and altruism. They have speculated that gamma rhythms relate to an expanded consciousness and spiritual emergence.

CONCLUSION

It is now known that even those who have become lazy in their mental habits can improve the circuitry of their brain. While there are many programs that are specifically designed to train your brain's circuitry, simple things like using your less dominate hand, playing cards, and doing puzzle books can encourage your brain to function at optimum levels.

For those who are serious about developing their brains, it is important to know which circuit of the brain you favor so that you can train the weaker circuits. If you are a logical person who prefers the executive function circuit, then making a point to list all the possibilities before making a decision will help open the creative circuitry. When you add selections that include the feelings of other people, then you are opening the awareness circuit, as well. If you are creative person who favors the creative circuit of the brain, then setting a focus and sticking to those parameters will strengthen the executive circuit of the brain. When you add selections that include yourself, and your personal limitations, you will also strengthen the awareness circuit in your brain. For the super sensitive types who primarily use the awareness circuit, then setting strict goals as you move through crowds will allow you to move about without feeling every emotional wave that is floating through the air. When you add the understanding that you and your agenda is as important as anyone else's, then you are able to disengage from the random drama that is happening within your environment and get on with the business at hand.

When you find ways to integrate the circuits of the brain, by including elements from all three circuits in your decision-making, you are developing the corpus callosum. The corpus callosum is key to optimal brain functioning because it is the bridge that links the brain circuits. Such development creates integrated functioning of the brain circuits, which could possibly be the explanation for the gamma wave. Finding the win-win, in every situation, is the way of the mystic and it will also bring you to a higher state of being.

In the next chapter we will see that attitudes and perceptions are just as powerful as the neural pathways and brain waves.

CHAPTER FIVE
THE CONCEPTUAL MIND

We have now entered into the area of the subconscious mind. The subconscious mind is special in two ways. First, the physical body in combination with the events of our lives creates all that is harbored in the subconscious. Secondly, it is also the foundational level of the spiritual essence. Since the spiritual essence is manipulated through thought, it requires an intense concentration that is not interrupted by judgments or issues from the past. A mind that is filled with issues, and cannot be still, cannot develop the ability to manipulate the spiritual energies. This is why the masters insist that the mind must be clear of thought before any advanced mystical training can begin.

No longer can we use tools, such as a thermometer, to measure a physical metric that is common to all humans, like the body's temperature. Our moods will brighten when we discipline the body, but simply changing our physical routine will not cleanse our minds of the issues that are buried in the subconscious. Unlike the body and the hard-wired brain, which are located in the physical sphere, the conceptual mind is quite the trickster. We have allowed the mind to judge without restraint. We have allowed the voices of our past to harass our self-esteem. So, being aware of thoughts and actions as they occur is key to catching the mind in the act of delusion.

Our perceptions and judgments are the focus of this facet. Changing the way we perceive other people and the events of our lives involves untangling the incidents of the past that now color the way we view the world. We will find that there is no black and white when it comes to personal beliefs. Belief can vary widely from person to person and from one culture to another. The social conditioning that we were all exposed to, even amongst those who lived in the same household, is not always the same.

Our minds capture experiences from the moment we are born. This helps us learn and process information quickly. However, it can also harbor cultural perspectives and negative events that cloud our judgment, which can cause us to react in inappropriate ways. The true mystic strives to clear these issues and harness the mind instead of allowing it to drag them along for the ride. You will have to face your demons and take responsibility for your problems. While experiencing the mystical states is quite nice, mysticism is not about escaping reality. For many, using spiritual practices as a means of escape is the roadblock that keeps them from the highest mystical attainments.

From the moment we are born, we are imprinted with experiences.

An experience includes the chemistry of the emotional body, the circuitry that is being utilized in the brain at that time, and the event itself.

For example, take a group of people who have seen a Broadway play. Even though there are thousands of people who see that exact same play, each will experience that play differently because each person will have their own unique chemistry, their own unique brain patterning, and all their previous history that shapes the experience they take away from that event. Once we realize that the number of variables in the equation that creates the psychological outlook is astronomical, we can understand that every person who has walked upon this planet, from the dawn of time to the present, is unique.

Each experience builds upon the next, creating both habits and a complex view of the world. These habits are not just actions but they can also drive habitual flow of the emotional chemistry through the neurons and the habitual way the information moves through the circuitry of the brain. All this activity begins with a random thought, which can then transform into a perception, and if the same conditions continue, it can crescendo into a fully formed belief.

When we start to look into the conceptual mind, we find that it is made up of innumerable thoughts, perceptions, and beliefs. No one begins this process with a clean slate. We all start with a crazed mind that the Buddhists have nicknamed, "Monkey Mind," because it is constantly jumping from one idea to another and babbling continuously. Ninety percent of what we consider real is actually a mental concept created by past events combined with the circuitry of the brain and the chemistry of the emotional body. True reality just "*is*" and lives outside of our personal judgments of what is good and bad.

For me, the message that my mind was out of control did not come as an image of wild monkeys. One of the first images that popped into my head, as a new meditator, was an image of a Wild West stagecoach pulled by a team of Clydesdale horses. The carriage was stalled while all the horses where running wild. Most of the team was still hitched to the carriage but each horse was trying to do what it wanted without respect to the other members of the team. Some were trying to forcibly drag the others in one direction or another, while others were sitting on their hindquarters and resisting with all their might. Then, there were still others that had broken free and were in the distance eating grass and refusing to help out with the situation. It was at that time I realized that I needed to train my team. I needed to get them to line up and run in the same direction. It was then that I knew that I could not blame others, or my circumstances, for my inability to move forward in life. The chaos in my inner world was causing the mess in my outer life.

You can see that the meaning, which is that the untrained mind is chaotic, was the same as the Buddhist "monkey mind" analogy. The cultural flavor of my upbringing created a very different image. This concept will be very important when we move on into the highest realms of the spirit, where we will be interpreting the writings and scriptures of the mystics. We will find that the exact same meaning can be narrated by very different symbols.

Once I started working on disciplining my habits and training my subconscious, there was no turning back. I didn't know it then, but this was the defining moment that was the turning point of my journey. I would become a mystic. Now, lets be very clear. A mystic is not some kind of wizard that has special powers to see the future or the ability to change reality.

A mystic is a person who has conscious control of themselves.

It is important to note that the classic way to decipher the workings of the subconscious mind is through dreams, projections, and visions. Remember in the previous chapter that the circuitry of the imagination is able to move in both directions? An image can create a thought. Or, the thought can create an image. This concept is fundamental not only to dissolving issues, but also in imprinting specific concepts into the mind. The subconscious is non-verbal. It speaks by producing images and feelings. When we dig through the subconscious, we find that it will send us messages through sensations and images. The ancient cultures valued these *"signs from God."* They designed complex rituals to entice the subconscious to produce a dream or vision that a priest or master could interpret. Just as my vision of a mind in chaos is different from the traditional Buddhist analogy, so too are the differences between cultures. The same message can be conveyed in innumerable ways. When interpreting a dream or vision, it is vital to grasp the basic message and not get hung up on the cultural nuances. We need to ask, "What is the basic message that the image is trying to convey?" It could be a complex picture that is simply telling us to stop or go. Or, It could be as simple as a flower that symbolizes the complex process of pollination that brings fruit.

In the subconscious realm, images do more than just describe our inner state. We learn that our thoughts and attitudes are as powerful as any action. The image of a luscious bowl of ice cream can motivate us to leave the comfort of our living rooms, drive ten miles, just to acquire this treat. This is the basis for the concept that an action in the physical realm begins with a thought.

While diet, exercise, and rest are the foundations of the physical realm,

Thought and attitude
are the underlying principles
of the spiritual realm.

Disciplining our thoughts and attitudes is required if we are to master the subconscious mind. This is the only way to dissolve the issues of the past that cloud the reality that we currently see. According to Yoda, "You must *unlearn* what you have learned."

When we first start digging into the subconscious, it can seem to be an overwhelming task. The mind races to judgment and, like a parrot, continually recites the negative statements of the past. The good news is that this whirlwind of craziness can be tamed by using the same methods that caused the current mess. That which has been imprinted, can be overwritten. Once we find a belief that has no value to our wellbeing, we can overwrite it with conscious messages. When we catch ourselves judging ourselves, or others, we can consciously reverse that habit by overwriting it with a positive affirmation. The habitual, "I am stupid," becomes, "I am a valuable person who is still learning everyday." This changes the watercolor painted by the emotional body. With practice, it is possible to move from a dreary scene of negativity into one filled with sunshine and hope.

Another way to bring change to our attitudes is to dig into specific events. We can doggedly pursue the cause and meaning that underlies a memory that still stings many years later. The critical evaluations of an elementary school teacher can be bottled up in a flashbulb memory that causes personal problems later in life. Once that incident is examined intensely, the bubble breaks and the pain from that event is then released. In that moment, a new view of the world comes into focus. When we understand that emotional pain is just a chemical response to an event, then we can allow the pain to come and go without fear. It then becomes possible to see the truth of the event and release the negative perceptions that clouded our judgments.

The mind has another unique quality. It cannot tell the difference between an imagined event and a real occurrence. This can be both a benefit and a hindrance to spiritual growth. Our world is filled with fear, suspicion, and violence. It is not just video games and movies that are to blame. The evening news shows more gory scenes than the average R rated movie. While there are numerous incidents happening throughout the world, at any given time, it is important to remember that even the most notoriously violent event is just one incident that involved an infinitesimally small percentage of the world population. It is very easy for the mind to imagine that we live in a completely unsafe world, when in fact; we live in a time that is safer than any other in human history.

Commercials insinuate that you will never get a date if your teeth are not white or if you do not drive the newest vehicle. What causes the emotional chemistry to fire? The musical sound track leads the way. Try watching a very dramatic moment in a movie with the sound turned off. Notice how your feelings do not engage with the scene in the same way. Once you understand that music can be a way to imprint your mind, it is important to examine the music you sing or listen to on a regular basis. Discipline your musical tastes to include only positive and uplifting messages for your mind to absorb.

There are many spiritual practices that use the imagination to imprint a variety of images and beliefs. Visual meditations, where you concentrate on imagining a calm environment that is recalled with a word or short phrase, can be very useful when you encounter a stressful event. The engrained patterning of the peaceful visualization can be called up with just one word, which deactivates the stress response. When these practices are correctly integrated into the spiritual routine, the mystical student benefits. Using images of the devil and the fiery abode of Hell to dominate populations or create fear are, unfortunately, very common. This is why it is so important for you to know yourself and understand your inner patterns. Then you will be able to discern what practices are beneficial for you and which ones you should avoid.

We can also use an expanded awareness to root out engrained programing. Being aware of what we say and how we react to social encounters can guide us to the deeply buried issues in our subconscious minds. Here is where a journal is extremely helpful. Instead of blaming someone else for our actions, we can turn inward and ask ourselves why did we snip back at a friend? Why did we feel the need to outmaneuver an associate's story with one of our own? Why did we grab that bag of candy when we mentally knew we did not need the sugar or the extra calories? What is it that causes us to do the things that we do? What are we trying to avoid? What comfortable situation we trying it recreate?

At a recent family gathering, my entire family was sitting in the living room, enjoying each other's company, when the sky opened into a torrential downpour. The conversation turned to what everyone liked to do when the weather turned nasty. The general consensus amongst my children was that when it stormed they have the desire to put on a movie and pop up a big bowl of popcorn. They were shocked when I told them that I purposely imprinted that into their subconscious. You see, when my children were little, I did not want thunderstorms to imprint a feeling of fear in them. So, when it stormed, all activities stopped. We popped up a big bowl of popcorn, put on a movie, and snuggled together on the couch. Then, when the thunder roared, we would all joyfully scream, "Boom! Boom! Thunder!" While they do not consciously remember any of these events, they still feel the imprint 25 years later. For them, when it thunderstorms it is time to snuggle indoors and watch a movie. Fear never comes to their minds.

You will not always have a warm and fuzzy memory that becomes conscious. Many times the memories that surface are filled with pain or fear that was not allowed to be experienced at the time of the event. This is a mechanism that the body and brain use to get us out of the bad situation first and then, when time permits, analyze the situation later. But when we are small, we do not have the faculties to debrief ourselves. So, these events are thrown into the back of the mind and must wait for a later time to be untangled. When we grow up in negative environments, we learn many tactics to avoid pain or to manipulate others to give us love and attention long before we are old enough to toilet ourselves. These survival tactics become deeply engrained and are extremely hard to root out of the subconscious but it is possible with dedicated work.

We are just as susceptible to the good feelings and perceptions we feel during a spiritual event as the bad feelings we experience during a confrontation with a bully. We look forward to attending a spiritual ceremony because it makes us feel good and opens our minds to wider realms of experience. This is not a bad thing, but we must be aware of all our motivations. We need to add a layer of logical control to our decisions. Does it feel good *and* is it good for our overall development? Euphoria is not always beneficial to personal development. Or does it feel bad *but* is what we need to change into a complete and aware individual? Sometimes we have to discipline ourselves away from the sweets and walk through the fire of negative experience. Each journey is different. Let's also remember, just because a particular experience was good for someone else's personal development does not mean that it will be beneficial for you and your personal development.

The benefit of mucking out the unconscious is that it helps our relationships, not just with others but also with ourselves. After a time of turning inward and analyzing our reactions to social cues, we come to see that everyone is reacting to subconsciously held beliefs. Instead of taking offense, we can see that we are not to blame for another's mood, attitude, or opinion. They are responsible for their perceptions and emotions, whether they take control of them or not. Now that we understand how the subconscious mind works, we know how important it is to deal with each incident as it comes. We understand that we need to take the time to analyze the events of our lives so that they do not create a rotting mess that will overflow into our relationships.

Please understand that it might not always be possible or beneficial for you to go through this process alone. Do not rule out the possibility of seeking guidance from a professional counselor or licensed therapist. The mind is like a house of mirrors. Navigating through the distorted images of our past can be very difficult. It could be that the memories are so intense that you need to unlock them slowly, and in a measured way. There is no shame in contacting a professional councilor or licensed psychologist to help you through the process of clearing the subconscious mind of its negative content.

There are many facets to psychology. It is just not possible to cover the entire gamut in this book. Here is a very brief run down of how the mind functions along with some of the built-in games the mind likes to play.

THE MIND'S GAMES

SEEKING CONNECTIONS

A deep sense of belonging is built into our human nature. A mounting pile of data suggests that we are shaped by our social environments and suffer greatly when our social bonds are threatened or severed. Science is realizing that social connection is not a luxury. Humans are born completely helpless. We need constant care for an extended period of time before we can take charge of our own needs. This means that we need to connect with our caregivers and be accepted by the tribe in order to survive. This is the basis for our need to seek connections, which is the first and deepest issue in our psyche.

When we experience cruelty in our social relationships, it feels as real as physical pain. We even use metaphors like "stabbed in the back" and "broke my heart" to describe the way it feels when we are socially attacked. Our brains behave as if we have been physically threatened when we are offended or excluded from the group. Avoidance of this pain is the reasoning behind why we allow ourselves to be influenced by the beliefs of others. When we have similar beliefs of those around us, we experience a social harmony that benefits everyone, ourselves included.

Here is where the need to be liked and be like everyone in our community comes from. We are continually enticed into conforming to the norms of our community or feeling that we must keep up with the Jones'. If we do not understand this built in mechanism that was essential for survival when we were first born, we will be sucked into every cultural belief and marketing scheme. We must decide how far we are willing to compromise. Simple matters of what is the right and wrong way to treat another person can become complicated when you follow the crowd and do not stand up for what is right. There is a famous study done on college students who were divided into guards and prison inmates. The experiment had to be stopped early because the conformity of the groups got out of hand. This happens time and again. We know that what we are doing is wrong, but since everyone else is doing it, our ingrained belief that we need to be part of a group makes it hard to break from the current norm.

Stereotyping, shunning, and outright hating those who are not like us is the negative extreme of this built-in need. We become so engrossed in the greatness of our own tribe that those of other tribes are considered inferior or dangerous. This belief is deepened with every experience because we are actively looking for evidence to confirm our convictions. This can make every person we meet guilty until proven innocent. It can take multiple encounters with people who do not fit into the stereotype of your clan to change your attitude toward those who are different.

SELF-ESTEEM

Self-esteem has two parts. It is the tendency to experience yourself as being capable of coping with life's challenges and feeling worthy of happiness and love. Your self-esteem is built, or rebuilt, according to the way you treat yourself and the way you talk to and about yourself. It is an active process of treating yourself well and replacing negative or self-critical thoughts with acceptance and realism. The way to raise your self-esteem is to face your problems head-on, while respecting your personal limitations. The feeling of self-confidence that comes with self-esteem is the result of hard work. Every time we accomplish a goal, it gives us one more thing that we can add to our achievements. As the list of achievements builds, we are willing to try a wider variety of activities. When we have a higher level of self-esteem, one set back will not discourage us from trying again.

SEEK PLEASANT/AVOID UNPLEASANT

We touched on seeking the pleasant and avoiding the unpleasant in the last chapter. A portion of the reason why we seek the pleasant is done in an effort to move toward a chemical balance in the brain. However, in some cases, seeking pleasure has nothing to do with the body's chemistry. We have a tendency to avoid the things that would bring a greater harmony to our lives because we have negative perceptions of the activity. The only way to treat this milady is to change the attitude. We avoid things, like the basic chores around the house because we perceive chores as *work*, which is the opposite of fun. Anytime we judge, we create a conflict within ourselves. Taking responsibility for our actions requires discipline. The easiest and fastest way to change our perception of a chore is to change it into an activity.

When we truly want to have a clean and organized home, it is important to make a commitment to that outcome. Only then, will we will be willing to do the work to make a clean home a reality. If we continue to live in our daydream world where some activities are considered good and some are considered bad, then life will continue to be miserable. A happy attitude is a *choice*, and not a result. We will never be happy if we think we must wait for the right combination of circumstances to fall in our laps. We can be just as happy doing the household chores as playing in the park, maybe even more so, if we set our minds toward the benefits of getting the housework done.

AVOIDANCE STRATEGIES

We all make mistakes. There are two ways to cope with our mistakes. We can tackle the problem head on and fix it or we can avoid the situation in a number of ways. The key to changing our behavior is to accept the responsibility for our actions and our emotions. We cannot change the behaviors that cause us grief until we are consciously aware that we do them. Once we accept responsibility, then we can work to change the way we behave. There are a number of ways that a person can refuse to accept the blame for their actions.

DENIAL - Refusing to acknowledge that what we are doing is wrong or hurtful because it is too uncomfortable to accept responsibility for our actions. When in denial, a person is unconscious of the reality of their actions. The way to change the unconscious to the conscious is to accept responsibility for the things we do. This can be a painful process because when we become aware of our faults, our ego is hurt.

Denial comes in many forms. We can minimize the effects or results of an action by making it appear less harmful than it may actually be by saying things like, "I wasn't drunk, I just stumbled a couple of times." We can justify what we are doing by making it look like a logical choice in the current situation by saying something like, "I had an especially bad day so I needed to eat that ice cream." We can, also, blame others for our actions by saying things like, "I wouldn't have done [that] if you had not done [this] to me first."

Denial can also include refusing to understand the harms that a behavior has caused others. This type of denial enables us to avoid feeling guilty and if it persists over a long period of time, it can prevent the development of remorse or empathy for others when we make poor decisions.

Denial of cycle is when a person does not take responsibility for the decisions that lead up to the event. Many times you will hear, "It just happened." Taking responsibility means that we must be responsible, not just for the event itself, but also for all the decisions we made leading up to that event. Take for example that your job allows you to have twelve sick days a year. On several occasions, you decide that you will call in sick when you were not really sick. Then one day, you really do get sick but now you do not have any sick days left. Your boss fires you for going over the maximum number of sick days allowed. The boss did not fire you for being sick. The truth is that you chose to waste your sick days. So, you must now take responsibility for your actions and accept the consequences. When we take responsibility for our actions, we learn that it is possible to circumvent tragedy before it happens.

Then, there is the denial of denial. Denial of denial means that a person is so unaware of the impact of their behavior that they believe that nothing needs to be changed. It is next to impossible to change a behavior when it is believed that nothing is wrong.

DEFLECT OR PASS THE BUCK - Is a combination of denial and blaming someone else. Questioning the observation of the accuser by saying, "Are you sure I said that? I don't remember it happening that way," is a common way to pass the buck. Have you ever played the game, "Who stole the cookies from the cookie jar?" The game goes around the room accusing someone of stealing the cookies. The accused then denies the theft and blames someone else. The game only ends when the group gets tired of playing. This game demonstrates not just the method of personal deflection but also how closure for the entire group cannot take place until culprit accepts responsibility for their actions.

ANGER - When we are angry, we feel powerful. So on one hand, anger feels good. On the other hand, if I get angry, then my anger will scare you so you won't make me accept my faults. This method of avoidance is similar to when an animal puffs itself up to intimidate the enemy. It is a scare tactic and method of domination. You will find that a person who uses this method of avoidance never learned the finer art of negotiation and compromise. They never left the "terrible twos." They bully and control others to keep from feeling uncomfortable emotions or accepting responsibility for their faults. This is not the way to cope with negative feelings or those who point out our faults. The responsibility of managing our emotions and behavior sits squarely on our shoulders. A true mystic does not force other people to behave in ways so that we don't feel angry.

"JUST KIDDING" - Is now considered emotional abuse. Not because it hurts a person physically, but because it hurts a person psychologically. Science is finding that the body will eventually heal, but the emotions will remain broken until they are consciously processed. The natural thing to do when our actions hurt someone else is to apologize for our behavior and to not do that again. When we say, "just kidding," the blame is placed on the victim instead of the person who caused the emotional distress. The situation is turned around and instead of the perpetrator accepting the responsibility for their actions; the victim is accused of being over sensitive or too uptight.

ISOLATION - This tactic uses our inborn need to connect against us. This method is used as method of psychological control. Threatening to kick someone out of the group is a nasty form of psychological manipulation. Rejection is quite painful, both physically and psychologically. When the wound is deep enough, it can cause the victim to turn to vengeance, and on some occasions, outright violence.

DELAYED GRATIFICATION

Delayed gratification involves regulating the self. It is the ability to resist a smaller immediate reward so that we can receive a larger or more enduring reward that comes later. Similar skills such as patience, impulse control, self-control, and ability to plan ahead are linked to a person's ability to delay gratification. The ability to wait for a greater reward is the mark of emotional maturity and is a factor in achieving an accomplished life.

The limbic system, which is the reward center of the brain, will always react to stimulus that can bring us a potential instant pleasure. The way to override this instinct is for the executive function, which is the reasoning and rational part of the brain, to be active and strong. Strengthening the executive function of the brain, so that it can contemplate the options, will reduce the temptation. Reminding ourselves of the dangers of an activity or thinking upon the greater reward we will receive later helps when we are faced with a tempting prospect. This type of distraction is a common way to increase the ability to delay gratification. When we allow our emotions to degenerate into impulsive or unconscious reactions, then we miss out on greater rewards that would have come if only we had had the patience and will power to wait. Clinical studies are showing that those who have developed the skill of delayed gratification report higher wellbeing, greater self-esteem, and openness to experience. They also report that the people who are able to delay gratification use productive ways to control anger and other frustrations. The good news is that self-control can be strengthened by practice. Once the benefits of delaying gratification are realized, then there is a powerful reason for a person to work for continued change.

TRAINING THE CONCEPTUAL MIND

The conceptual mind is the home of strategic thinking. It is a blend of the imagination circuit and the executive function circuit. Foreseeing future consequences of present actions is the foundation of strategic thinking and planning. The imagination is used to create a desired outcome, while the executive function is used to develop and implement an action plan that will result in bringing the imagined outcome into the physical world. The ability to think strategically is closely associated with the density of connections that are housed in the corpus callosum.

In this type of planning, the creative circuit takes center stage but it must incorporate executive function parameters such as time, money, and the availability of resources. The executive function circuit is enlisted to set goals, determine what actions are needed to achieve those goals, and mobilize resources to execute those required actions. Only a mind that has eliminated its issues is clear enough to tackle the multifaceted dynamics of strategic thinking. Since the imagination circuit runs in both directions, strategic thinking comes in two forms: design and invention.

DESIGN

Design is the forward thinking strategy. The outcome is imagined first. Then the plan for bringing this item into the physical realm is then put into place. In this form of strategic thinking, the final product is known. You will find this form of strategy used when creating anything from an architectural plan, a fashionable interior, landscape, new fashions, and event planning.

In this form of strategic planning, the designer creates, let's say, a dress that will be part of her next collection. The designer will use her imagination to envision this new dress. She will then have to work within the parameters of the human form, which means she will need to provide buttons or zippers so that the garment will allow access for the arms and legs. She will need to be cognizant of the genre of the dress, such as evening wear. Last but not least, she will need to understand the dynamics of fabrics and the availability of notions, like thread, ribbons, and buttons. Once the design is sketched, it is then put into production. Production for a runway showing includes the measurements of the model, who will be wearing this dress, when it is presented to the public. In this case, the design dictates all subsequent choices.

INVENTION

Invention is a backward thinking strategy. It begins with a problem. The outcome is the solution to that specific problem. Invention merges known things, known ideas, and known processes together to create something new that serves a purpose or fulfills a need. In this case, the final result is unknown. It does not matter what the solution will look like. What matters is that the problem is solved, within certain parameters. Let's say that we are again creating a dress, but this time it will be an invention.

Once the problem is identified, the first step is to select the parameters. We will need to determine how much time we have to complete this project and how much money we have to spend. The next step is to gather together what we already have and what we need to complete this project. In this case, we were able to acquire a couple of dresses from a thrift store, another dress was donated from a friend, and a few accessories that we already had. With a little sewing skill, we are able to create a new dress using parts from the other three dresses. As you can see, the available options will dictate the outcome.

CONCLUSION

Strategic thinking requires training. Juggling multiple goals, within interconnected parameters, hones the brain's ability to think strategically. It is very simple to lay out a route that will get all the errands completed in an efficient way. Now throw in that Johnnie has to be at karate practice at 5:00 and picked up at 6:30 and Sarah has to be at dance at 5:30 and picked up at 8:00. It becomes quite a mental exercise to fit in all the stops and still hit the timed appointments on schedule. Then, when you add the upcoming events over the long term, the mind truly has to plan and use time strategically to get everything done. Any kind of psychological issue will disrupt the integrated flow of the mind. Drama and emotional upset shuts down the logical mind, which leads to wasted time and energy. While there are fabulous courses and great games to train your mind, do not down play life's lessons. In many cases, the events of your everyday life will be your greatest training. Who knew that loading the dishwasher, so that the water spray will hit every dish, could be a great way to train the brain?

We have barely scratched the surface regarding the ways a mind can distort the truth. When we act from a truth that is twisted by unprocessed issues or cultural bias we create situations and circumstances that make life difficult to navigate. When our minds are engaged in emotional turmoil, we have little brainpower to visualize and plan our future. When we continue to run away from our issues, we waste time that could be used to build a better tomorrow for ourselves and others. Those who have taken control of their body and mind are well adjusted and most likely successful. They can think strategically and create from either direction.

But, if we want to become a true mystic, there is another realm that requires our conscious control. The next layer of development involves the spiritual realm. We will explore the practices that have been handed down through the spiritual systems of the world. We will discover how they affect the bioelectrical field of the soul, which in turn affects the physical realms of the body and the mind. At this time, the bioelectrical energies are too subtle for science to measure. Yet, we have 7,000 years of observational data that describe, in symbols and metaphorical stories, the underlying framework of the bioelectrical field of the soul.

The Realm
of the
SPIRIT

CHAPTER SIX
THE PRACTICES

The realm of the spirit is the home of the bioelectrical field of the soul. This realm is purely vibrational. Like a piece of music, it cannot be seen but it can be felt. At this time, science is not able to precisely measure the human energy field. The only way to know or understand how your bioelectrical field functions is to experience it for yourself. Here is where we unwrap the mystery that has been the exclusive knowledge of the mystics. The active facet of the spirit contains the spiritual practices, while the passive facet contains the laws and the framework of the bioelectrical field.

From the beginning of known human history, every culture developed methods to lead their people to the experience of the divine. Each civilization has given us unique insight into how to experience the bioelectrical field through their spiritual beliefs and religious practices. As we find in the next chapter, it is important that the practices you participate in meet the criteria of bringing *your* body, *your* mind, and *your* spirit into balance. This is why randomly selecting practices or following a religion just because our family has done so for generations can lead to disastrous consequences.

As we found in the previous chapters, you are uniquely you. The practices that bring you into balance and harmony with your bioelectrical field will be a unique mix. Some of us need to build self-esteem. Some of us need to manage stress. Some of us need to expand our creative capacities. You will be creating an Individualized Education Program (IEP) that maximizes your potential for personal development. Affirming that, "I Am powerful and worthy of all good things," is a practice that is beneficial for those who need to build self-esteem. This affirmation works by overwriting the negative messages that are housed in the unconscious mind. Affirming that, "I Am powerful and worthy of all good things," is not beneficial for someone who begins the path of personal development with a bloated ego because this practice will work to further inflate the ego.

With the exception of Taoism and many indigenous spiritual systems, this spiritual facet is understood as the flow of a single spiritual energy. The missing link to mystical development is that the realm of the spirit is a bioelectrical field. In order for an energy field, of any kind, to exist there must be two energies, one positive and one negative. You will find the references to these two energies in every culture from the beginning of time. The Taoists call them Yin and Yang. The Christians call them The Bread and The Wine. The Chinese call them The Dragon and The Tiger. The ancient Egyptians and Sumerians called them The Sun and The Moon. All of these names are referring to the same two energies. For the sake of this book, we will use the most common names that are found in the spiritual texts from around the globe and throughout time: Water and Fire.

The Water and Fire energies have principles of operation that are seen in a majority of the mystical texts. The elemental names hold within them a basic understanding.

Water falls down.

Fire rises up.

When we connect the images and stories of Father Sky and Mother Earth to the Water and Fire energies, it is possible to unlock the understandings of the ancients. While there are exceptions, for the most part, the Water energy was associated with Father Sky and the Divine Masculine principles, while the Fire energy was associated with Mother Earth and the Divine Feminine principles. We will dig further into the principles of the Water and Fire energies as part of Mystical Law #2 in the next chapter.

Harmonious motion of the bioelectrical field requires continuous maintenance. It behaves like a tuning fork. The vibrations of the bioelectrical field will weaken and die if they are not continuously activated. This is why most religions require that members attend a form of worship on a regular basis. Regular practice keeps the energies of the bioelectrical field of the soul in motion.

Each practice was originally designed to enhance or initiate the flow of a particular energy. We will discuss which energy is activated during each practice. As you try new practices, it is important to document your feelings and whether your progress is positive or negative. For the first week of any new practice, take time to write down not just the practice itself, but also how you felt and how you behaved immediately after doing the practice, an hour after the practice, several hours after the practice, and how you felt the next day before undertaking that practice again. For instance, if you are seeking empowerment and self-esteem, then note if the practice helped you get through the day or if it just added to your exhaustion and hopelessness.

Not always will a practice make you feel euphoric. In many cases, euphoria is not beneficial to personal development. There are many who use spiritual practices to escape reality. Being drunk on God can be just as detrimental to your life, and the lives of those around you, as being drunk on alcohol. The desire for everything to be fun, happy, and pain-free is a trap that our minds set. We must break away from the idea that life will somehow be all candy and kisses.

It is also important to understand that spiritual practices have a tendency to bring up the issues of our past and make us aware of the consequences of our behaviors. These feelings can be uncomfortable. When this happens, it is important to face the issues that are being presented. Once faced, the issue will dissolve and is less likely to cause future negative behaviors or emotional suffering. Sometimes, it can take multiple trips down the same road before we can fully heal an issue and accept ourselves as unique individuals.

So, when you evaluate a practice, don't throw out a practice simply because it causes uncomfortable feelings. Evaluate the practice by how well you recognized the issues, as they arose, how quickly you moved toward an authentic reaction, and how long it took to recover your natural balance after an event. You can reduce the time and the intensity of the practice if things seem overwhelming. Remember, you are in control of your personal development.

A spiritual practice should never make you feel so worthless that you become hopeless to the point of suicide or so arrogant that you knowingly hurt others without remorse. If you experience either of these types of feelings:

STOP THAT PRACTICE IMMEDIATELY!

Note which energy was initiated by that practice and change to practices that initiate and strengthen the opposite energy.

If you are working with a spiritual teacher or guide, contact them and tell them your experience. If they do not respond in ways that validate your experience and help you rebalance your bioelectrical field, then disassociate yourself from them. A beloved guru, who knows only one of the two paths, can destroy the inner being of students whose bioelectrical fields require an energy that is different than the guru's to attain balance. Those students never progress even when they diligently follow the teacher's instructions. They become completely dependent upon their guide, never realizing that they are sinking deeper and deeper into dependency instead of becoming independent. These spiritual guides are not bad teachers, but what they are teaching is bad for *you*.

It is important to understand that a practice is still valid and worthwhile even though that practice is not right for you. Banning a spiritual practice, or any religion as a whole, deprives those who need that philosophical viewpoint from attaining the highest levels of personal development. It would be like banning Type B blood at the blood bank. Type B blood is not bad in and of itself, but it is bad if it is administered to those who have Type A blood. That is why it is important for the blood bank to stock both types of blood. It is important to note that before the blood bank dispenses any treatment each patient is tested for blood type, which ensures that the type of blood that is administered is compatible with that person's internal structure. The same process of testing to make sure that a practice is right for you should be followed whenever you try a new spiritual practice.

No guru or spiritual councilor can do the work for you. A teacher or guide can point the way and advise you as to the practices that will benefit your progress. It is your responsibility to, first, become aware of and, second, control your bioelectrical field. There is no maximum level. Advancement is determined by how much work you put into your personal development. There is no use in going to an energy master if you go home and do all the same things that put you out of balance in the first place. You will become dependent upon the healer and never learn to manage your energy, yourself.

Spiritual practices serve two purposes. First, they activate one of the three realms of the being. We have seen that fasting is not just a spiritual activity. It is a scientifically proven way to optimize the way the body functions. In many cases, you do not have to subscribe to a particular faith to participate in many of the practices. Second, they initiate and enhance the flow of a particular energy. We have already delved into the physical benefits of many of the practices. This chapter will seek to bring understanding of the energetic significance of each practice.

CONCENTRATION MEDITATION PRACTICE

Concentration practices enhance the Water energy. These practices build focus and concentration, which strengthens the executive function circuit of the brain. In this style of meditation, the mind is not allowed to wander. Practice begins with selecting an object of focus. It is like putting blinders on a horse so that activities that are outside of the forward focus do not distract it. Each time the mind wanders away; it is gently guided back to the same object. By diverting the mind away from the dramatic reruns, a creative personality type can learn to shut down the emotional rollercoaster that negative mind chatter creates. These strategically placed meditations will train the brain to stay focused on the business at hand, allowing the creative personality type to stay focused, finish projects, and meet deadlines.

AWARENESS MEDITATION PRACTICE

Awareness practices enhance the Fire energy. These practices expand the intuition and jump-start the creativity, which strengthens the creative circuit of the brain. In this style of meditation, the mind is trained to be inclusive. The brain is challenged to include as many variables as possible. Practice begins by opening the mind. Thoughts are then allowed to pass like clouds through a summer sky. When we find that we have become entangled in a thought or sensation, we redirect the mind to reopen to the widest view. When we start to see the endless possibilities in the small moments of our lives, we are then able to train the brain to look for these possibilities everywhere.

MASTER PRACTICES

Breath Work, Meditation, and Walking are the three practices that are found in a majority of religions and belief systems. I call them the master practices. Secular professionals like medical doctors, life coaches, professional councilors, and psychologists regularly recommend these three practices to their clients and patients.

These practices, as well as many others, can be manipulated to enhance either form of energy. There are two ways to change which energy is initiated or enhanced. The first way is to adjust the objective of the practice. If we wish to enhance the Water energy, we need to do concentrative or mindfulness practices. On the other hand, if we want to initiate the Fire energy, then we need to open our minds to awareness or transcendental style practices. The second way to change the energy that is initiated or enhanced is to simply change the way we breathe. We will be discussing the importance of breath work in the next section.

It is time to delve into the practices. We will evaluate each practice with an eye to which energy each practice enhances or initiates. There are complete books on spiritual practices and it is not possible to include them all. We will start with the three master practices and then move onto the most common practices of each realm.

BREATH WORK

The breath is a major part of every facet of personal development. Everyone knows that the breath brings oxygen to the body. What most people don't know is that it serves as a disconnect for the emotional system, an object of concentration, and the means to circulate the spiritual energies.

The first step in any breath work practice is to return the breath to its natural state. Breathing deeply from the belly will bring more oxygen to the body. This will energize the body and improve the level of functioning. Don't be fooled by the simplicity of this practice. This is much harder than it seems! Stressful situations cause us to breathe shallowly and over time shallow breathing becomes a habit that is hard to break. Take time each day to notice your breath. Are you breathing deeply or shallowly? If you notice that your breaths are shallow, redirect the breath deeper into the belly. You can do this anywhere. Remind yourself to notice the breath while waiting in line at the store, while sitting at a stoplight, or between the activities of your day.

The next lesson in training the breath is to modulate it into an even rhythm. When we get excited or stressed, our breath becomes uneven and jagged. Jagged breathing is a form of breathing that is similar to gasping for air. Gasping heightens the stress inducing chemicals that flow through our bodies. When you take time each day to train the breath, redirect the breath to be deep, even, and smooth. Practice as often as you can so that deep and even breathing becomes the norm for your body.

In many belief systems, the abdomen is considered the reservoir that holds the body's energy. The deeper you breathe, the more energy is stored in the belly. This energy is used throughout the day when we do physical labor and when we are mentally engaged in creating and problem solving. The greatest drain on our energy reserves is emotional turmoil. As we have found in chapter three, breathing deeply can disengage the emotions by turning off the fight or flight chemistry in the body. Practicing this body hack will bring down emotional misery and stop the needless waste of the bioelectrical energies.

The Taoist tradition calls the breath, "the bellows." Breath is the pump that circulates the energies through the body. The way you breathe determines which energy is pumped through the bioelectrical system. While there are sophisticated practices that can move the energies in and through specific areas of the body, we will only be touching on the basics. If you are interested in the deeper teachings, you will need to become a student of a qualified energy master.

The Water enhancing breath brings understanding and Peace. It is recommended for those who are creative and whose brains function primarily along the creative circuit.

Warning! Intellectually minded people, whose brains function primarily along the executive function circuit, will be harmed by these breathing practices. Zeus and Thor carried lightening bolts as weapons of mass destruction, not vehicles of blessing.

The Water breath consists of breathing in through the nose and out through the mouth. It is like a big sigh. The focus of this breathing practice is to pull the Water energy from the top of the head and push it down to the ground. In general, the exhale is longer and stronger than the inhale. This breath is calming and soothing. With practice, you will be able to feel the Water energy flow down through your system, like a stream or waterfall. Like the rivers of Eden, the bioelectrical system begins at the top of the head and flows down in four different directions: down the back, down the front, and down each side. When your mind is clear, it is possible to direct the energy into any channel you choose. In this way, you can consciously bring Water energy to any part of the body.

The Fire enhancing breath brings compassion and Love. This breath is recommended for those who are intellectual and whose brains primarily function along the execute function circuit.

Beware! This practice can be very dangerous for those who are creative and whose brains primarily function along the creative circuit. If you work too hard at this style of breathing you can cause fierce headaches and black out from hyperventilation. This style of breathing naturally activates the adrenalin in the body. Depending upon your biological and mental makeup, it can make you feel either energized or anxious. It can, also, pump up the desires into mania if it is not carefully monitored.

The Fire enhancing breath consists of breathing in through the mouth and out through the nose. The focus of this breathing style is to pull the fire energy up from the ground and push it up into the head. The inhale is typically longer and stronger than the exhale. So, if you find yourself being lazy, this breathing style will kick you in the pants and get you up off the couch. Here, the focal point resides at the base of the spine and flows up in four different directions: Up the back, Up the front, and up on each side.

The next suggestion is to crisscross the breath. Consciously circulating the breath so that it crisscrosses through the body and the brain will help to build and strengthen the pathways in the corpus callosum. The corpus callosum connects the creative and executive function circuits so that the brain can engage in the higher functions of thought. Practices, such as breathing through one nostril and consciously breathing during yoga or qi gong twisting practices, help to facilitate the crisscross of the breath.

The final recommendation revolves around the energy movement practices. Yoga, tai chi, qi gong, and the marshal arts involve movement and poses. While these practices do stretch the muscles and remove tension in the body, the greatest benefit comes when the breath is integrated into these practices. It does not matter which energy you are trying to enhance. It is important that you do a complete inhale and a complete exhale before moving to the next pose or movement. This will fully push the energy through the channels that are being opened by the poses and positions.

MEDITATION

Meditation has been in use since antiquity. It starts as a way to expand the mind or calm the emotions. As awareness grows, it develops into a technique to experience the movement of the bioelectrical energies. Once the energies are identified, it then becomes possible to manipulate those energies in ways that maintain balance in the body, mind, and spirit.

Quieting the mind is the first level of meditation. It is the basic training of spirituality. Until we train our minds, it will behave like a spoiled toddler. It will babble on about inconsequential things. It will chase after every new object. It will whine and cry when life presents any circumstance that is uncomfortable. It will become enraged, which pumps the fight or flight emotional chemicals into the body, when it is offended. Keeping the mind in check can seem to be an impossible task.

The techniques that train the mind to be like a tranquil lake *seem* very easy when they are explained. However, we all are shocked at how much ruckus is going on in the mind when we first begin to meditate. The beginning practices of concentrating on the breath, letting the thoughts pass without engaging in them, or visualizing a simple scene are extremely hard practices because your mind has been allowed to run wild up until now. It is like training a puppy or small child. Repetition is the key to success. It is important not to consider yourself a failure if you cannot get the mind to stop its crazy antics during your meditation session. We do not give up on a puppy when it potties in the house. So, we should not give up on ourselves when we can't keep our thoughts from jumping from one thing to another during our meditation session. It is important to keep working until we reach a point where we have some control over our thoughts. Once we have control over our minds during our meditation sessions, we then move to taking control of the mind in our everyday lives.

Any activity can become a meditation. The moments spent waiting for the microwave to ding or waiting in line at the store can become a valuable meditation session. There are great benefits to breaking your meditation time into smaller chucks. The beginner will find it easier to accomplish a full meditation session, while the experienced meditator will benefit from bringing meditation out of the meditation hall and into daily life.

Your mind is like a puppy.
It will not learn a skill the first time it is presented.

Meditation needs to be consistent and done on a regular basis. Training works best when it is practiced multiple times throughout the day. Each meditation session ingrains the intent of the training. When you notice your mind chasing another rabbit, do not fight it or criticize yourself. Gently call your puppy-mind back to your favorite meditation object. Over time, mastery of the mind can be achieved.

Meditation that influences the bioelectrical field of the soul can only take place when the mind is clear. It is important to have a disciplined mind and be clear of our issues to manipulate the bioelectrical field. It is possible to manipulate either energy through meditation by changing the breath. Visualization, in unison with the breath, can move either bioelectrical energy. A prime example of this is the white light meditation. You begin by visualizing a white light that is streaming down from above your head. During meditation, you allow this light to enter through the top of the head, flow down into all parts of the body, and then pierce the ground. You can strengthen the meditation by synchronizing the Water breath with the downward flow of the white light. It takes a very long time to achieve sufficient concentration for you to visualize this complete process. So, don't be discouraged if you cannot accomplish this meditation in the first couple of tries. The rising of the Fire energy can be achieved in the same way by visualizing a red flame rising through the body and using the Fire breath to enhance the upward flow of the Fire energy.

Meditation is separated into two types: concentration and awareness. Each of these types can be further segmented into breath practices, walking practices, observation practices, and silent mantra practice. Here is where knowledge of your personality type and brain circuitry will help you select the meditation style that will bring you the greatest potential for spiritual development.

WALKING AND PHYSICAL EXERCISE

The third master practice is walking. As we have seen in the previous chapters, walking affects both the physical and mental facets of the body. It also affects a majority of the mystical facets. Walking promotes circulation. Our bodies are constantly in motion and need motion to operate properly. Walking strengthens the muscles of the heart, lungs, legs, back, and abdomen. When we walk, the heart must work harder to pump the blood and the lungs are required to bring in more oxygen. These are not the only systems that circulate through the body. The lymph is another of the body's circulating systems. The lymph system is an intermediary between the blood and the cells. It acts as a waste receptor and harbors a large number of white blood cells that kill bacteria when they reach the lymph nodes. The lymph system does not have its own pump. The only way for the lymph to circulate through the body properly is through physical exercise.

Walking also helps the body manufacture its regulating chemicals. Mood enhancing brain chemicals, like dopamine, require exercise to be synthesized. Since many of these chemicals cannot cross the brain blood barrier, the brewing of the mood enhancing chemicals must take place in the brain itself. How is that accomplished? With exercise. Walking intensifies the movement of the bioelectrical energies and keeps the body humming. When walking is blending with the other master practices of breath and meditation, you have created the trifecta of personal development.

THE SPIRITUAL PRACTICES

It is hard to divide the practices into groups because the mystical system is multifaceted. Each practice has the potential to affect all the other aspects of the system. I will discuss the spiritual practices according to the realm that they primarily benefit. You will need to discern the sublime effects for yourself.

The length of time you practice, your current level of attainment, and energy that you are channeling through your bioelectrical field determines the outcome of any practice. There is no maximum level. Advancement is determined by how much work you put into your personal development.

PRACTICES OF THE BODY

DIETARY RESTRICTIONS – many spiritual systems have food restrictions. These restrictions generally stem from the lack of sanitary conditions in ancient times and can include prejudice against peoples who ate specific food items. But these types of restrictions have little to do with mystical transformation. Dietary restrictions, like vegetarianism and high protein diets, do affect the functioning of the body chemistry and the mystical matrix as a whole.

Vegetarian diets ramp up the Fire energy within the bioelectrical field. The lack of complex proteins and fat, which takes much energy for the body to burn, allows the Fire energy to rise up with little restriction through the mystical matrix. It is like burning dried leaves and grass. A fire that is fed dried leaves and grass immediately shoots up as it easily devours the fuel that is added.

High protein diets have the opposite affect. Protein takes much energy to burn, and keeps Fire energy occupied in the lowest regions of the bioelectrical system. This allows the Water energy to fall downward and dominate the mystical system. Now we know why Jack Spratt could eat no fat and his wife could eat no lean.

SPIRITUAL FASTING – is an extreme reset of the body's chemistry and energy matrix. The most common use of this technique is when a student is initiated into a belief system. It is also used as a means of cyclical renewal and as a method to hurtle yourself up to the next level of attainment. With the removal of all food, the Fire energy is allowed to rise up unrestricted. This opens the third eye chakra, which activates the creative centers of the brain to produce images and visions. *This practice is not recommended for those with creative personalities that primarily use the imagination circuit of the brain.*

RELAXATION TECHNIQUES – reduce the stress that is held by the body. From a mystical point of view, stress is an over abundance of the Fire energy. Relaxation techniques drain the body of stress by bringing down the Water energy. Once the practitioner is able to connect the Water energy to the ground, there is what the Christian writings call, "the Peace that passes all understanding."

CHANTING/SINGING – is breathing on steroids. The rhythmic cadence of a song or chant will dictate the inhalation and exhalation of the breath. A song or chant has the ability to ramp up endorphin production as the amount of oxygen that is circulating in the brain increases.

Chanting and singing are vibrational. When you sing, the vibrations harmonize your brainwaves to the frequency of the song. You can open the creative centers of the brain with an alpha wave chant or put the baby to sleep with a delta wave lullaby. In general, the higher pitches entice the Water energy to fall and the lower pitched tones encourage the Fire energy to rise.

The words that are used, in a song or chant, are also significant. Repetitious phrasing overwrites previous experience. This is especially true when the vibrations of the song open the mind to the most receptive frequencies that reside in the ranges between 7 Hz and 8 Hz, which is the boarder between the Alpha and Theta brain wavelengths.

DANCING – is very similar to walking. It also promotes multiple circulations through the body. The difference is that dancing usually includes more of the upper body in its movements. Movement of the arms and the twisting of the torso encourage the energies to flow in multiple directions. Dancing requires greater awareness in order to be conscious of how the energy moves through the body. This practice can be used to bring up the Fire energy when it is sensual or rapid. It can also bring down the Water energy when it is slow and graceful.

CHANGING POSITION DURING WORSHIP – is both a mental and a physical practice. Changing positions from sitting, to standing, to kneeling, or prostrating changes the flow of energy through the body. The energy flow of the body is not the only realm that is affected. The mental state is also affected by the positions. Prostration promotes the attitude of humility, while standing promotes the attitude of confidence. Kneeling places the mind in prayer mode and sitting allows the mind to relax and receive the teaching given by the spiritual leader. Changing positions during a worship service also keeps the mind engaged so that the practitioner will not be tempted to fall asleep during worship.

WORK/WORKS – many cultures believe that the way to keep the "Devil" away is through work. Work burns off the Fire energy that naturally rises within the bioelectrical system. Since you are using the Fire energy in positive ways as it arises, it makes it less likely that you will experience an excess of Fire energy that can manifest as rage or mania.

PILGRIMAGE – is extreme exercise. The Fire energy is activated by the struggle to complete the journey. Pilgrims experience a wide variety of challenges when they take to the trail. The weather, terrain, and the distance combine to intensify the experience. The mental challenge is as exhausting as the physical one. There is no way to escape yourself when you are on pilgrimage. Talking yourself through completing that next uphill mile or keeping a happy composure in the rain puts the mind through basic training. The benefit of pilgrimage is that you learn to appreciate the little things in life. Simple things, like beautiful scenery, can make us aware of the grandness of creation. The end of the trail brings euphoria and pride in accomplishment along with the many lessons you have learned about yourself.

PRACTICES OF THE MIND

PRAYER – is a practice that raises the Fire energy within the bioelectrical system. In general, prayers are requests or promises that are made to a God above. It revs up the bioelectrical system and, in intensive and prolonged practice, can lead to ecstatic feelings. It is the same experience that a runner experiences after reaching the point when the brain produces excess amounts of dopamine, which is known as runner's high. The mind then tends to connect those ecstatic feelings to the prayer and subsequently to God. The Sufi scriptures refer to this as "drunkenness." There is much discussion in the Sufi writings as to whether it is better to be drunk or sober when doing the spiritual practices.

Here again, there is no right or wrong. You need to select practices that will balance your energy system. For the intellectual type, there is much benefit gained from a drunkenness that comes from destroying the structures of judgment and opening up to the expanse of the divine. Creatives, who already have access to the universal expanse, need to stay far away from this type of practice because they need to build structures that provide them with the ability to stay on task and to make discerning judgments.

The words that are repeated in a prayer are burned into the memory. They overwrite any previous experience and they become a focal point for understanding any new experience.

GRATITUDE – is the opposite of prayer. This practice encourages the Water energy to fall. The practice of gratitude shifts the brain into acknowledging the gifts that have already been received. Counting our blessings brings the mind into a positive state. It opens the awareness to a wider view of reality. No matter how bad the situation we think we are in, there are many who are worse off. The more often we look for the good in any situation, the better able we are to see the good everywhere and not fall into a attitude of negativity.

AFFIRMATION – is similar to gratitude. The difference is that an affirmation expresses gratitude for things *before* they have manifested in the physical world. We can affirm acceptance of ourselves as unique individuals. We can affirm that the universe is guiding us in every moment. We can affirm that our being is being nourished in every moment. Affirmations move the mind from understanding to knowing. When we say these things, that seem so outlandish to the intellect, the mind starts looking for proof. It is a way to trick the mind into seeking what is best for us. That which you seek, you will find.

CONTEMPLATION – is concentrating the thought on one thing. The object of contemplation can be anything. It can be a single object, like a candle flame, a passage from a religious text, or an experience in your day. Contemplation can be both expansive and contractive. On the one hand, it is a concentration style practice because there is only one object being considered, like the flame of a candle or a blade of grass in the yard. On the other hand, it can be expansive when you are trying to find all the angles of meaning within a passage that is located in a spiritual text. No matter what you contemplate, the goal is an understanding of the subject that is so deep that it becomes an experience in and of itself.

SELF-EXAMINATION – is contemplation of the self. Existential questions like "Who am I?" and "What is my purpose in life?" is the expansive side of self-examination. Such questions open the mind to the wider existence.

"Why did I say that?" and "Why did I feel offended?" demonstrates the concentration side of self-examination. Mulling over the events of the day helps us to understand our motivations and issues. It forces us to reach back into the depths of memory and find the things that are lodged there that prohibit us from being the best person we can be.

VISUALIZATION – opens the creative centers of the brain. When we actively create images, we are strengthening the imagination circuit of the brain. It is a way of training the mind to stay focused on one object. Once the object is created, an attribute can be attached, such as Peace or Love. Then, the object can be used as a way to circumvent the emotions. We can create a feeling of Peace or Love just by bringing up that image in the mind.

When further developed, it can be used to "watch" processes as they flow. It can begin with simple visualizations like imagining two gears when they are in motion. Once the imagination is honed, it can visualize a complete process. This is the primary skill used to move the energies through the body.

DREAM INTERPRETATION – examines the imagery that the brain is creating. In this case, the experiences, issues, and thoughts are creating images. We can use these images to dig deep into the subconscious and root out issues or explain behavior.

SYMBOLISM – is an image that has a standardized set of meanings. Since symbols are images, they cannot be understood through intellectual understanding. Interpretation requires that the creative centers of the brain become active. Complex images require the intellect to access multiple regions of the brain to find the meaning of the symbol. Everything from color, to number, to historical significance, to cultural perspective needs to be included in the interpretation.

Sophisticated cultures use layering to insure that the interpretation was properly understood. This means that they will use multiple symbols that refer back to the same meaning. For example, the cartouche of Psusennes I, who was dubbed *The Silver Pharaoh* by archeologists, included a star, water, bread, and a kite (a white bird that brought blessings from above, which is equivalent to the Christian dove of peace). When you add these symbols to the silver of the innermost coffin, you understand that this pharaoh considered the Water energy superior.

PRACTICES OF THE SPIRIT

GRACE – is the name given by the Christian faith to the Water energy. Worship that focuses on the Water energy usually takes place in a wide-open space that is filled with light. These worship spaces welcome everyone to enter. The best examples are Catholic Cathedrals. They welcome visitors and most provide tours when worship services are not in session.

KUNDALINI – is the name given by the Hindu faith to the Fire energy. The object of this practice is to force the Fire energy up to the crown chakra, which is located at the top of the head. The Fire breath is a very prominent part of Kundalini practice. Kundalini practices are usually done in small, hot rooms.

The ancient Jewish faith revolved around the worship at its temple located in Jerusalem. Entrance into the temple was segregated. As you move deeper and deeper into the more sacred parts of the temple, fewer and fewer people are allowed access. The inner most sanctum, known as the *Holy of Holies*, was entered only once a year, during the celebration of Yom Kippur, by the single most qualified priest.

BELLS, CHIMES, AND SINGING BOWLS – emit vibrations when played. The vibration is used to align the brain waves and the bioelectrical field to a particular harmonic. Each harmonic enhances the activity of a particular chakra, which governs a particular segment of spiritual transformation. The higher tones tend to activate the chakras in the head and neck. The tones on the lower register tend to activate the first three chakras in the lower levels of the body.

DRUMMING – is a Fire energy practice. It activates the Fire energy and helps it to move up the chakras. When the beat of the drum is slow, it activates the lower chakras at the base of the spine and in the lower abdomen. As the beat increases, it activates the chakras higher up on the central channel until the drumming is so rapid that the Fire energy reaches the crown chakra. Dancers, and even members of the audience, will experience a drunkenness and spiritual mania when the drumming reaches a fevered pitch.

QI GONG – was developed as a system to cultivate and balance the life energy with the purpose of healing the body. It is an art that primarily uses Water energy. Practitioners use very slow physical movement, breath work, and focused visualization to build energy that can be used to heal the illnesses of the body and mind.

Those who choose to become healers must be able to measure the energy flows in their patients. Qi Gong masters, for the most part, use touch to determine the energy flows because "seeing" auras and energies is an attribute of Fire energy masters.

TAI CHI – is another Water energy practice. Many consider Tai Chi to be a school within the Qi Gong lineage. It is considered an internal martial art. The slow movements allow the practitioner to distribute the energy through the different energy channels to achieve mental clarity and greater longevity. The Yin-Yang symbol used by Tai Chi represents the merging of the Yin and Yang energies into a single ultimate force. Focusing the mind on the movements brings clarity to thinking and calms the mind. There are five traditional schools of Tai Chi, which are: Chen, Yang, Wu (Hao), Wu, and Sun. Mayo Clinic calls Tai Chi a gentle way to relieve stress.

YOGA – was developed by the Hindu faith and is a Fire energy practice. It is defined as raising and expanding the consciousness from oneself to encompass everyone and everything. Yoga has many varieties, which include: Hatha-Yoga, Raja-Yoga, Mantra-Yoga, Bhakti-

Yoga, Karma-Yoga, and Kundalini-yoga to name just a few. Spiritual yoga practice includes ethical precepts, metaphysics, systematic exercises and self-development techniques for the body, mind, and spirit.

REIKI – is an energy healing practice that uses lightwork, which is another metaphor for the Water energy. While this system is spiritual, it is not part of any religion. The healer begins at the top of the head and moves down through the body aligning the energy as they move. It is used for stress reduction and relaxation, which promotes a feeling of peace and security as well as healing illness.

MARTIAL ARTS – are not just for building the physical strength and the mastery of the physical body. The earliest known practice of martial arts took place in the Xia Dynasty more than 4000 years ago. Many of the martial arts were founded by monks or nuns. Emphasis was placed as much on spiritual and philosophical development of the student as a preparation to defeat an enemy.

In the next chapter, we move to the laws and framework of the bioelectrical field. We will discuss the metaphors of the mystics and come to understand why it is important to choose the correct path for you and to stick with a set of practices that coordinate with that path.

The road runs both ways

CHAPTER SEVEN
THE BIOELECTRICAL FIELD OF THE SOUL

We have come to the pinnacle of mystical development. Understanding, feeling, and seeing the energies as they flow through the bioelectrical field of the soul is the highest achievement of a master mystic. The way to reach the highest levels of attainment is to bring balance to your energy system. In the previous chapter, we discussed which energy is enhanced, or initiated, by the different spiritual practices. In this chapter, we will discuss the process of change within the two systems of spiritual transformation. While each person will experience these changes in a unique way, there is a common sequence of change for each spiritual path. Understanding these processes will open the door to interpreting the metaphors of the mystical texts of every belief system.

As we look into the earliest known civilizations, we find that many of the ancient cultures honored Father Sky and Mother Earth. These two deities were personifications of the Divine Masculine energy of Water and the Divine Feminine energy of Fire. As the Divine couple, they worked together to create the world and kept the cycles of life in motion. Rain was considered to be the semen of Father Sky that impregnated Mother Earth, who then produced grain and other crops that rose out of the earth. Each year, the cycle of planting and harvesting would continue life on this planet. The ancients understood that as long as these two deities worked together in a balanced way, life would be prosperous.

When the ancients formulated their spiritual practices, they emulated the workings of nature. The ancients considered the gender of the body as the determining factor in choosing a spiritual path. They believed that the male body was naturally endowed with the Divine Masculine energy of Water. In order for balance to take place within a man's spiritual system, men were automatically assigned spiritual practices that initiated and enhanced the Divine Feminine energy of Fire. Fire energy warmed the heart and gave men the ability to be compassionate and caring.

The ancients, also, believed that the female body was naturally endowed with Divine Feminine energy of Fire. Since Mother Earth required the essence of Father Sky for her womb to produce food, the ancients assumed that the same process would be true for a human woman. As a result, women were automatically assigned spiritual practices that enhanced and initiated the Divine Masculine energy of Water. This helped women control their emotions and gave them the ability to multitask and think strategically.

The landscape of spirituality was forever changed when Zoroaster put forth his theology. Zoroaster moved away from a gender-based system of deities. He proclaimed that the Fire energy, which emanated from the rising sun, was all-good and the Water energy, which emanated from the moon on a dark night, was all bad. He was the first to use the metaphor of war to describe the transformational process. The apocalyptic battle between the Sons of Light and the Sons of Darkness was born. The old ways of balancing the Divine Masculine and Divine Feminine were abandoned. From that point in history to our present time, spiritual development has been considered a war between the forces of good and evil.

Zoroaster's philosophy was carried throughout the Mediterranean and the Middle East. It was fully adopted by the Jewish culture after their captivity in Babylon. Before the exile to Babylon, YHWH was worshipped along with his Asherah. Asherah was considered to be YHWH's wife and thousands of Asherah statues have been unearthed by archeologists in cities that pre-dated the Babylonian exile. After the exile, YHWH was considered the only deity worthy of worship. Later, when the Jewish tradition branched off into Christianity and Islam, the concept of The One True God, who was male, became the norm throughout the Middle East. The patriarchal revolution was now fully ensconced in the culture of the region. This meant that the only approved method of spiritual transformation was to kill the ego. From that point on, only the Fire path was honored as Holy.

While there are a few notable exceptions, women were unable to endure the initiation of Fire. The influx of feminine energy into a predominately feminine energy matrix overloaded their emotions and caused them to be filled with anger, desire, and mental insanity. As time passed, women were eventually banned from initiatory rites and spiritual leadership. In the ancient writings, we find that women are considered spiritually inept and undeserving of spiritual teaching. They were relegated to the outermost portions of temple complexes, which lead to a general classification as second-class citizens.

As time went by, the idea that there were two energies, that gave rise to two completely different ways of spiritual development, was buried and eventually lost. It is only in recent times that Carl Jung resurrected the philosophy that the inner being of every person contains both the animus, which consists of the masculine qualities, and the anima, which consists of the feminine qualities. Jung's philosophy resurrected the two elements of the inner being found in the ancient philosophies. He fully defined the death of the ego as a process where a man unites with the feminine qualities that were latent within him. The ancients called this process *The Way of the King* or *The Fire Path*. Jung's protégée, Joseph Campbell, who spent many years studying mythology from around the globe, dubbed this process of transformation, *The Hero's Journey*.

However, while Jung did understand that women needed to unite with their animus, he never fully defined that process. Campbell, too, stated that there had to be a separate transformational path for women. When asked if he could define the transformational path for women, Campbell commented that the spiritual path for women would have to be detailed by a woman. Since spiritual development must be experienced, he, as a man, would not be qualified to outline the spiritual path of women.

The concepts and the in depth study of these two men have brought back the masculine and feminine dynamic of the psyche that is contained within the ancient philosophies. This reopens the door to finding the twin paths that make up the universal framework of spiritual transformation. We see that the divine pregnancy of Mother Earth is not telling the story of a dying and rising god. It is the ancient spiritual transformational path for women. The birth of the divine male child marks the emergence of the animus, which provides a woman with the ability to use logic and think strategically.

While it is important to understand the gender designations in order to interpret the ancient writings and practices, current scientific findings call for us to update the way we determine who follows which path. We will be more interested in the functionality of the brain, specifically, whether your mind runs on the executive function circuit or the imagination circuit, as the determining factor for choosing a mystical path. Now, we can begin to reassemble the clues that the ancients left behind in their images, parables, and myths.

As with all physics-related sciences, the science of the bioelectrical field of the soul, also known as mysticism, has fundamental laws of operation. These laws are universal, which is why we find the exact same philosophies in cultures that never could have communicated with each other due to distance or time. The laws of mysticism are:

- **MYSTICAL LAW #1** – The One is found by balancing The Two.
- **MYSTICAL LAW #2** - The Principles of Water and Fire
- **MYSTICAL LAW #3** – The Two Transformational Paths
- **MYSTICAL LAW #4** – The Archetypes of Satan and Lucifer
- **MYSTICAL LAW #5** – Breath and Thought move the Energies
- **MYSTICAL LAW #6** – Water brings Fire and Fire brings Water
- **MYSTICAL LAW #7** – Water And Fire Annihilate Each Other
- **MYSTICAL LAW #8** - Know Thyself
- **MYSTICAL LAW #9** - Know Thy Student
- **MYSTICAL LAW #10** - Spiritual Texts and Symbols are Scientific Formulas

These mystical laws create the basis for understanding the bioelectrical field of the soul. Once these laws are understood, the mystical stories reveal the fundamental science of the human bioelectrical field as they were originally designed. When this knowledge is put into practice, advanced personal development is the result. It is time to explore the mystical laws and principles that govern the bioelectrical field of the soul.

Mystical Law #1 – The One is found by balancing The Two

The One is neither masculine nor feminine. It is a dynamic balance of the masculine and feminine energies. The One is found by consciously working to balance and merge the masculine and feminine energies that naturally flow through us.

In science, we know that when there are two energies, a positive and a negative that combine along a shaft that contains both a positive and a negative pole, it creates an electrical field.

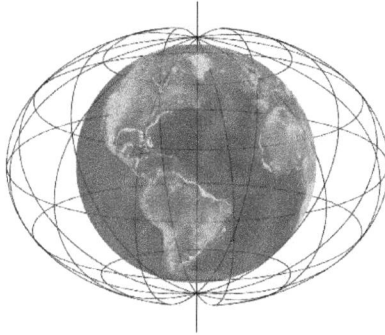

Our planet is a prime example. We know that the earth has a magnetic field. This field generates many conditions upon our planet. It is a dynamic framework that gives rise to a living system that influences everything from the heating of the magma core, the spin on its axis, the shift of the tectonic plates, to the global weather patterns and much more. It also holds an atmosphere in place that shields us from harmful solar rays. Without the magnetic field, all life would die and our planet would be as desolate as the moon or mars.

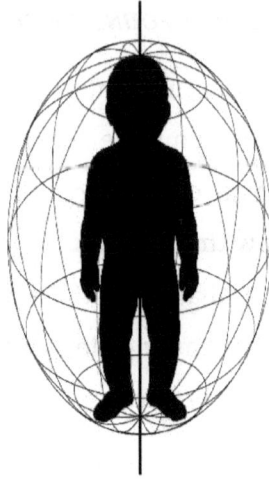

Our bodies are encased in the same type of bioelectrical field that envelops our planet. We have an energy field, commonly referred to as an aura, which resembles the layers of the atmosphere. This is the glow around the body that is depicted in paintings and icons of saints. This glow is visible to the naked eye when you have consciously worked to increase the energy that is flowing through your bioelectrical field of the soul.

We too have a central shaft that contains a positive and a negative pole. The Hindu faith calls this shaft the Sushumna. It is wrapped with two channels that direct the positive energy and the negative energy through the body. Hindu tradition has named these two primary energy channels the Ida and the Pingala. The Ida is associated with the Water energy that falls from above. The Pingala is associated with the Fire energy that rises from the ground. These two channels start on opposite sides of the Sushumna and move in a spiral, much like the DNA helix. They cross each chakra, or energy portal, as they flow through the body.

The movement of energy through this system keeps us healthy. That is why the symbol for the western medical profession is the caduceus, which is a central pole with two snakes wrapped around it.

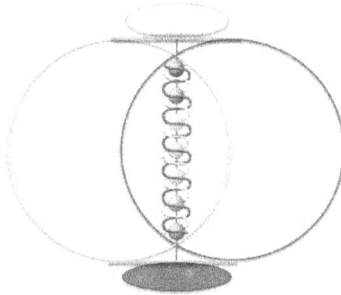

This diagram is a two-dimensional drawing of the bioelectrical field of the soul. It contains the blending of the masculine and feminine spheres, the central pole, the positive and negative energy channels that wrap around the central pole, as well as the chakras. You will notice that at the top and bottom of the central pole lies a pool of energy that can only be accessed by breaking the barrier that is holding it in place. This is the beginning point for everyone.

We all begin with a dominant energy that flows through our spiritual system. For some of us, the Fire energy is dominant. This makes us naturally caring. We think of others first and have a mindset that is creative and is open to blending ideas, processes, and philosophies from different genres. For others, the Water energy is dominant, which leads to having a naturally logical mind. Their minds are geared toward linear thinking and judging situations from the standpoint of how this will benefit a specific purpose. There is nothing wrong with either way of being. However, to be a mystic, who is a whole person that can choose the most beneficial view point depending upon the circumstances of the situation, the creative person needs to develop focus and discernment and the logical person needs to cultivate compassion and expansive thinking.

The spiritual texts tell you that the objective of mysticism is to merge with *The One.*

The way to merge with The One
is to bring balance to the bioelectrical field of the soul,
which means you must consciously do practices that
increase the latent energy within your spiritual system.

When I was studying the multitude of religions, I noticed that different cultures strengthened different energies. The energy that was revered and initiated by the spiritual practices was not the same in every religion. Some religions celebrated cleansing the chaotic mind and giving birth to the divine within by bringing down the Water of Peace. While other religions, insisted that the way to wholeness was to kill the ego by bringing up the Fire of Love or compassion.

For many years, I wandered through the philosophies wondering which way was right and which was wrong. I observed that many people were psychologically destroyed by the practices that killed the ego. I also read stories of people who followed the way of giving birth to the divine within, only to become the most arrogant narrow-minded people who abused those who did not fit into their idea of what was right or good. In both cases, something was wrong. It was then that I realized that there are two energies at work within the spiritual system. That meant there were two different ways to achieve a balanced spiritual system and two ways to overload the spiritual system into dysfunction.

The Combination of Energies

	WATER	FIRE
w a t e r	**W**w Lucifer	**F**w Birth of the Divine
f i r e	**W**f Death of the Ego	**F**f Satan

This chart shows the combinations of the two energies. The dominant energy is in capital letters while the latent energy is in lower case. Notice that there are two ways to balance, which means that both energies are included. These two ways represent the two basic spiritual paths. The Wf combination has the Water energy as the dominant and the Fire energy as the latent energy. This path works to kill the ego, by enhancing the Fire energy. This path is commonly known as *The Hero's Journey*. The ancient Sumerian *The Epic of Gilgamesh* is a classic example of this path. The Fw combination has the Fire energy as the dominant energy and the Water energy as the latent energy. This path works to give birth to the divine male child by initiating and enhancing the Water energy. Christianity's *Nativity Story* and Buddha's *Flower Sermon* are classic examples of this path.

This diagram also shows the two ways of unbalance, which means that the bioelectrical field of the soul is overloaded with a single energy. The ancients depicted these combinations as Satan and Lucifer. Satan was traditionally depicted as a female demon that was possessed by the need to kill and destroy all life. Lucifer was depicted as a male demon of cold arrogance and selfishness. When monotheism took control of the Western world, the Light was deemed fully good. Once that happened, there was no room for an evil entity that was pure Light. It was at this time that the entities of Satan and Lucifer were merged.

Each religion makes the mistake of assuming that everyone begins with the same dominant energy. In the West, it is believed that every person is under the influence of a malevolent ego that needs to be killed. Initiating and enhancing the Fire energy kills the ego. This is all well and good when the dominant energy in the spiritual system truly is Water. However when the dominant energy in the spiritual system is Fire, practices that initiate and enhance the Fire energy only serve to unbalance the spiritual system by overloading it with more Fire instead of bringing balance between Water and Fire. I have come to this understanding:

*In the greater scheme of the universe, there is no wrong path. But, there is a wrong path for **you**.*

Now, we can reach back in time and excavate the knowledge that is found in the ancient writings. Archeologists have found great treasures but they have not been able to decipher the complete meaning of what they have found. The modern philosophy of only one God, who is male, has blocked even the most adept scholars from fully understanding the ancient inscriptions and texts that are speaking of a One God that is a dynamic blend of the masculine and feminine.

Energy theory and energy healing is not a New Age fad that was thought up in the last couple of centuries. Energy systems and energy healing have been part of the human experience for over 5000 years. Proof of this comes from the remains of a man that archeologists have named Otzi the Iceman. His mummified body was found in the Otztal Alps on the border between Austria and Italy, in September of 1991. Otzi had sixty-one tattoos. The markings have been identified as either acupressure or acupuncture points that would relieve the pain of his deteriorating spine, hip, and knee joints. This is not just speculation. The scientists have come to this conclusion because the markings on Otzi's body and the current symbols used in acupuncture have changed very little in 5000 years. This means that energy healing, in the form of acupressure and/or acupuncture, was practiced and well known on the European continent 2000 years before the earliest known use in China.

MYSTICAL LAW #2 – THE BASIC PRINCIPLES OF WATER AND FIRE

The forty-second chapter of the IChing states that the Original One begets The Two. The Two that is referenced in this doctrine are the positive and negative energies that work together to create the bioelectrical field of the soul. The Taoists call these two energies Yin and Yang. These two energies are mutually dependent upon each other. Both are present in every moment. What makes each moment different is the relative balance between the two. Just as there are many shades and tints of purple, each moment will be a unique combination of these two energies and can be metaphorically defined as the different hues of purple.

To function at its optimal potential, your bioelectrical field requires that the positive and negative energies be in balance. It is the balance of these two energies that makes it possible to merge back into the original One. Once balanced, the process of personal development is to gradually increase these two energies. So, let us examine these two energies and understand the principles that each contain.

FIRE

This energy is hot and spins to the right as it rises up from the ground. It is associated with the color red or black and is expansive. The ancients, who lived before the time of Christ, were keen observers of nature. They associated this energy with Mother Earth. They believed that Mother Earth emitted an essence of Fire and so this energy was deemed the Divine Feminine. It is easy to see why these connections were made every time we watch a fire leap higher and higher into the air as it moves from being a small ember into a roaring blaze or observe a volcano as it explodes and hurls molten lava up into the atmosphere. The Fire energy, which is generally warming and beneficial, has a fury that is destructive when unbalanced or uncontrolled.

The Fire energy is equivalent to the Hindu Kundalini energy and the ancient Roman concept of The Christ. It warms and sweetens as it rises up within a Water dominant spiritual system. Fire ignites the emotions and strengthens the imagination circuit of the brain. It brings forth passionate Love, which is the basis for breaking down the barriers and judgments that prohibit relationship. This energy is known for its ability to cut away all previous judgments and attachments by expanding the awareness. As it flows, it opens the heart and rips through every belief that was entrenched in the mind. Many texts report that the initiation of the Fire energy feels like the rumble of a devastating earthquake or sounds like the thunder of horsemen who ride across the plains, wreaking destruction, and permanently altering one's way of life.

Fire is the positively charged energy within the bioelectrical matrix. It is also associated with the color gold and the golden sun that rises in the east. Just as experiencing the dawn of a new day can bring feelings of being renewed, the initiation of the Fire energy can bring the feeling of rebirth into a new way of life. In many traditions, once the Fire energy is initiated, the initiate is given a new name to celebrate the beginning of this new life.

As we learned in a previous chapter, the mind creates pictures in order to make sense of transcendental experience. The most common forms seen by the mind's eye can be: blood or a river flowing with blood, wine, a serpent, a fiery cross, a red rose, a burning bush, a burning arrow of love, a sword, the Holy Spear, an erect penis, complete destruction followed by a complete renewal, or the agony of crucifixion.

WATER

The energy that is symbolized by Water is cooling and spins to the left as it falls from above. It is associated with the colors white, clear, or iridescent and is contracting. The ancient peoples associated this energy with Father Sky. As the essence of the Father, this energy was deemed the Divine Masculine. The cooling nature of this energy gives the feeling of being chosen or blessed. The Water energy, which is generally nourishing and peaceful, has a tendency to constrict, which can produce judgments of good and bad when unbalanced.

The Water energy is equivalent to the Christian concept of Grace and the Buddhist theories of Light. It enlightens and organizes as it falls within a Fire dominant spiritual system. Water solidifies the intellect and strengthens the brain's executive function circuit. Understanding and clarity creates a structured approach to thinking and this is the foundation for reining in a chaotic mind. The result is a Peaceful existence. This energy is known for its ability to narrow the focus and constrict the awareness to the business at hand. As it flows, it limits the number of variables, which allows the mind to use the creative qualities in strategic ways. The spiritual texts report that the initiation of the Water energy feels like water flowing down through the body or a Light that glows either in the head or throughout the body. The ancient Egyptian tradition used a robing ceremony, where the initiate was dressed in a white robe, to denote the full attainment of the Water energy. Christians call this moment *The Transfiguration*. The Buddhist tradition calls this experience, *Enlightenment*.

Water is the negatively charged energy within the bioelectrical matrix. It is also associated with the color silver and the silvery moon that casts its glow downward in the nighttime sky. Just as experiencing the full moon on a quiet evening can bring a feeling of Peace, the initiation of the Water energy can bring a feeling of a Light that shines in the darkness.

The most common mental images that are associated with the Water energy's transcendental experiences are: Rain, snow, lightning, light, a stream or river, a chalice, a bowl, bread, Manna, milk, moon, star, semen of Father God, a white flower – White rose, White Lotus, Edelweiss, the pollination process that causes vegetation to bear fruit, or pregnancy and birth of the divine masculine within the Self.

MYSTICAL LAW #3 - THE TWO PATHS

Now that we know that there are two energies that make up the bioelectrical field, it makes sense that there are two ways to balance the energies. It is now possible to understand why some people thrive while other people are damaged by any one religion. Both paths use the same initial structure. The difference between the two paths of transformations is dictated by the direction of the transformative energy.

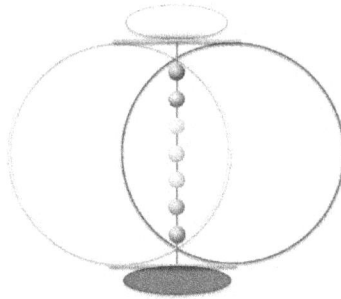

Here is the basic structure of the bioelectrical field as envisioned by the Hindu faith. It contains the Water sphere of energy and the Fire sphere of energy, the inner sanctum, which is the intersection between the Water and Fire spheres, the chakras or energy gates that make up the ladder of spiritual progression, the entryways into the spiritual realm, as well as the respective pools of Fire and Water energy. This is the beginning phase for everyone.

Now that we have seen the basic structure, let's take a look at the two spiritual paths.

THE FIRE PATH

The Fire path is known by many names. The ancients called this transformative path the *Way of the King* or *The Warrior's Path*. As we said earlier, Joseph Campbell named this path, *The Hero's Journey*. Those who followed this path were known as, "the ones who see." In the Christian theology, the events of Holy Week and the Crucifixion symbolize the progression of the Fire path. We can also comprehend the progression of the Fire Path in the stories of Moses who experienced the burning bush and unleashed the ten plagues upon the Egyptian peoples. In ancient times, only men were initiated into this process of personal transformation. The purpose of initiation is to open the gate at the base of the spine to start the upward flow of the Fire energy. As the Fire energy moves from the base of the spine to the top of the head, different aspects of your life will be brought into awareness. Past issues are brought to light and encrusted mental perceptions are remapped as the creative areas of the brain are opened. Over time, any wall that prevented an open mind is destroyed.

Once the flow of the Fire energy is initiated, subsequent practices are intended to increase and enhance the Fire energy and to incite it to rise through the bioelectrical system. The Hindu tradition has fully mapped this process with its system of chakras and the rise of the Kundalini energy. The chakra system describes seven levels. Each level is comprised of different aspects of the psyche. As each chakra is cleansed, the initiate becomes aware of their issues. This can be a painful process, which is why the process along this path is sometimes called, "the *path of tears*." It is unfortunate that many ancient texts portray the process of clearing ones issues as a battle against demonic forces. Sadly, this metaphor continues to give religious groups justifications to attack other groups, who do not believe as they do. The true way of attainment, which is to command a particular spiritual level within your own psyche, is to clear the issues within your own spiritual system. Not to make war on other peoples.

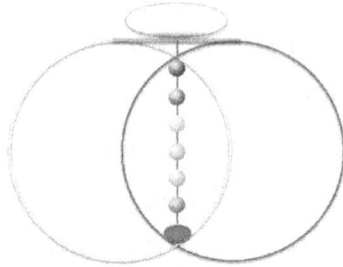

The first level is where the basic survival instincts are disciplined and refined. As you can see, the entryway at the bottom of the drawing has been opened and the Fire energy has risen to encompass the lowest chakra. Awareness is brought to the body's basic needs. Diet, exercise, and proper rest are analyzed and changed. Fasting is a common method used to reset and control appetite. Breathing is retrained so that it is deep and even. As the Fire energy moves up, it opens the mind to the next level of awareness.

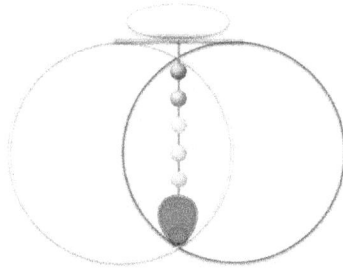

The second attainment involves desires and basic creativity. The Fire energy has now moved up to fill the second chakra. We become aware that what we do today affects the events of the future. If we constantly cave into the desires of the present moment, then we will not achieve our long-term goals. If I don't go to work, then I don't get paid. If I hit someone, they will hit me back. As we begin to see the consequences of our actions, we stop blaming others for our circumstances. Taking responsibility for our actions can be a very uncomfortable realization. Be gentle with yourself. What you knew in the past is not what you know today. Morality and upstanding behavior are the lessons learned. Sexual energy is controlled and redirected instead of released in fits of lust.

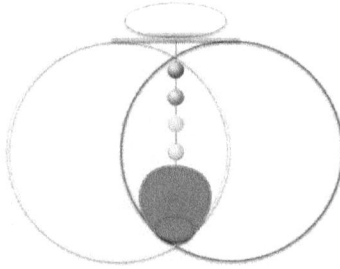

The third attainment involves personal power. Instead of overpowering others, power is now directed toward doing good in the world. Dictatorship evolves into leadership. A great leader does not dictate conditions or demand adoration. Great leaders bring out the best in others and build teams of people who trust and care about each other.

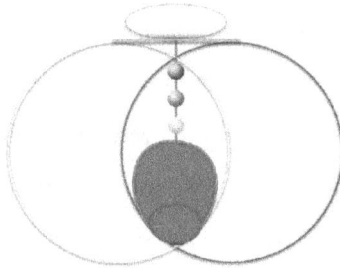

The fourth attainment is when the Fire energy reaches and cleanses the heart. A sweetness and love fills the being. It can be described as luscious warmth that makes you drunk with ecstasy or it can be described as a flaming arrow that rips the heart open. Either way, caring about, and for, others becomes a part of life.

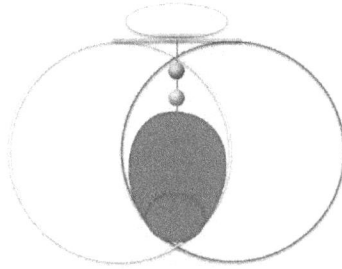

The fifth attainment makes us aware of the power of our words. Words can hurt and they can heal. We become aware of the words we use. We realize that by just changing a few words, we can change the outcome of a conversation. The emotional response to vibrational inputs becomes apparent. We learn that it is not just the words but also the tone of voice. We become aware of the emotions evoked by music. We learn how to use music to keep ourselves in a positive emotional state. Lessons in morality are revisited. This skill is not to be used to manipulate others for your own gain. The goal of every mystic is to become a beneficial presence to the surrounding community.

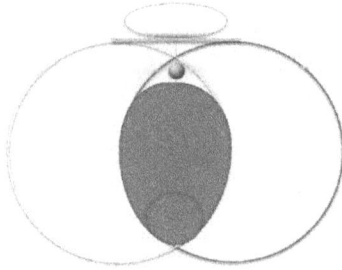

In the sixth attainment, we become strategic. The litmus test for this level of attainment is, "What am I creating?" We understand that we do not have to wait until we can complete the whole project in one sitting. We understand that if I write one hour each day, then, in time, my book will be published. Small increments of time, that were previously wasted, are now productively used. When we find ourselves with a few minutes of extra time, we look for the small things that can be done now that will benefit the outcome of the project down the road. The ability to mentally disassemble and reassemble objects or processes and strategic planning is the focus of this attainment.

In ancient Egypt, Imhotep, an architect from ancient Egypt, was worshipped for many centuries after his death. The reason he was worshipped was because he envisioned the first pyramid. The ancient Egyptians wrote everything thing down. We have everything from court documents and official accountings to grocery lists and love letters. While we have found papyrus with the mathematical theories detailing the proper angle of the pyramids, we have not found a single architectural plan. Imagine being the architect of a colossal building project at a time when there was no such thing as an architectural plan. The plan, complete with each detail, was held in the mind of the architect. Many of the world's greatest minds, like Albert Einstein, were able to mentally envision mathematical equations or scientific theories.

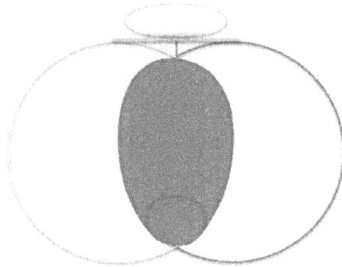

The seventh and final level of attainment is the expanse of space. It is described as a blackness or void. The veil of separateness is lifted as we realize that everything that has manifested into this reality relies upon the interplay of innumerable factors to come into existence. We can now connect the dots and see that the situations and circumstances surrounding key events shaped you into the person you are today. We can be grateful for our struggles and even thank those who caused us harm. This path of transformation creates the archetypical righteous and compassionate hero or king.

THE WATER PATH

The Water Path runs exactly opposite to the Fire Path. The ancients referred to this path as *The Grail Path* or *The Virgin's Path.* Those who followed this path, in ancient times, were known as, "the ones who hear," because they could feel deeply. Feelings were associated with vibration, which is the basis for hearing. In Christian theology, the story of *The Nativity* symbolizes the experiences that take place along this transformational path. The Taoist tradition gives us *The Secret of the Golden Flower.* These stories arise from the agricultural understandings of the time. They relate to the process of pollination, where insemination takes place on the wind or from a male god who resides in the heavens. The culmination of this path is to bare fruit or give birth. This path shows us why Jesus cursed the tree that did not bear fruit and why Buddha gave the famous lotus flower teaching, which consisted of simply holding up a white lotus flower. In ancient times, only women were allowed to travel this path. Early Roman law prohibited any man from entering the cult of the goddess. Men, who ignored this regulation, lost their citizenship and were shunned.

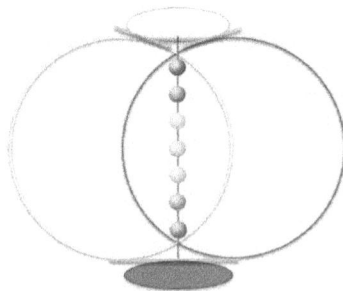

The purpose of initiation is to open the gate at the top of the head and start the downward flow of the Water energy. As the Water energy moves from the top of the head to the base of the spine, different aspects of your life will be brought into awareness. Understanding and knowledge remap the mind as the intellectual areas of the brain are strengthened. The first step of transformation is to open the gate at the top of the head. This ceremony was traditionally called *The Wedding.* In this ceremony, the female initiate became connected to the expanse of the universe by marrying the male deity. She then was able to experience the Oneness of creation. Today, as in ancient times, marriage is a legal contract. Both the bride and groom make vows to a committed relationship that supersedes all physical conditions. We find that this practice continues today when a Catholic nun takes her vows. She is married to Christ and vows to remain in a committed relationship with the divine for the rest of her life.

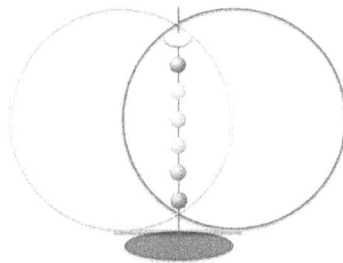

Comprehension of the interconnectedness, complexity, and synchronicity of life brings the initiate to a sense of awe and wonder. The initiate comprehends that everything in this world comes into existence through the interplay of innumerable factors. This understanding prepares the initiate for reviewing the aspects of their own lives. Transformational development is a process of accessing buried memories, understanding the situations and circumstances surrounding key events, and realizing the wonder of how those things, even the traumatic, made you into the unique and beautiful person you are today.

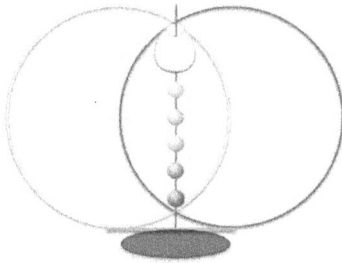

As the Water energy flows downward, it opens the chakra known as the third eye. The second attainment gives the ability to see patterns in nature, replay the situations and circumstances of life, as well as see the energy flows within ourselves. As you will see, this ability has applications and uses other than creating fantasy. The ability to "see" processes is a skill that can be sharpened. Albert Einstein had a special name for the ability to use the imagination to play out consequences. He called it, "mind experiments." He had honed his mind to such a clear state that he could mentally picture the processes and outcomes of his mathematical equations. Once you achieve a high level of skill envisioning systems at work, then all systems are open to you. This is how designers can visualize a finished remodel from bits of flooring and scraps of fabric. The third eye is not just the seat of design, strategy, and system processes, but also the seat of Karma.

The Hindu belief system states that Karma is the backlash of happenings that you put into motion. If you are generous, then others will be generous to you. If you take from others, then others will take from you. Understanding the outcome of your actions *before* you do them is key to keeping negative Karma at bay. The Taoist concept of Wei wu Wei, which means action without reaction, teaches students to think before they act so that anything they do does not cause a backlash of unwanted events.

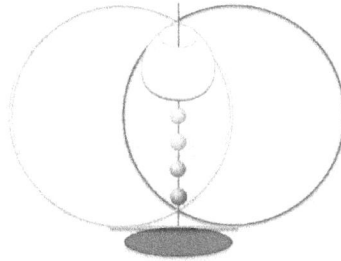

The Water energy continues to flow downward, building mental structures and filling each space with the light of understanding. This attainment governs the mouth and the ear. It is the home of generating and receiving vibration. Speaking sacred words and syllables is a common ritual practice. Vibrations from prayers, chants, and singing set the tone of a ritual space. This is why many faiths require that ritual or ceremony be performed in a set space, on a regular basis. Just as the vibrations of a tuning fork will slow and eventually cease when it is not continuously played, the holiness of a space will fade over time when ritual or ceremony ceases.

The vibrations don't just sanctify the ritual space. They also sanctify the worshippers by harmonizing their bioelectrical field to the frequency of holiness that is within the ritual space. Blessings that are intoned by instruments or spiritual masters can be received and incorporated into the inner being. This attainment gives us the ability to feel the ambiance of a ritual, a space, or a holy person. A common way for a spiritual master to impart Water energy to disciples or spiritual students is through a kiss on the mouth. When the Water energy reaches the throat chakra, it physically feels like a kiss. The bridal kiss, or the Kiss of God, was considered a sign of this spiritual attainment in antiquity.

Another aspect of this attainment is not just the morality of lying but also the realization of who we are. That which comes out of your mouth is all about your personal inner world. The issues and congealed thought patterns that are harbored in your mind will spill out through the words you say. Here is where we understand, "That which you speak of, is what you are." Once we grasp this understanding, those little tell tale Freudian slips can be used as barometers of the soul. Keeping a log of your conversations and then reflecting upon them will give tremendous insight into what needs to be healed within your own psyche. The flip side of this realization is that this truth is the same for everyone. That which comes out of someone else's mouth, most probably, has nothing to do with you. A person will see and criticize in others what needs to be healed within themselves. This is the basis for the psychological concepts of perception and mirroring.

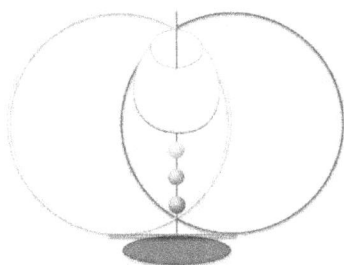

We now move into the area of the heart and the world of relationships. The first person that we need to establish a positive and loving relationship with is ourselves. An open heart allows us to bless misfortunes and forgive the missteps that have shaped us. We find the unlimited capacity to see the good in all things and to love, regardless of situation or circumstance. Here is where Love is infused with Logic. We find that love is about giving that which will benefit the recipient, not only in this moment, but also in the longer term. We see that completely protecting and providing every need is very loving when it comes to infants. However, such behavior creates long-term psychological damage when young adults are over-protected and not required to stand up for themselves, rely upon their own resources, and accept the consequences of their actions.

The followers of the Water path know that to spread negativity will bring negativity back to them. They also know that atmospheres of emotional turmoil dissipate the Water that has accrued within the bioelectrical field. Those who follow the Water path understand that compassion is about giving understanding and encouragement, not pouring more sorrow or drama into an already emotionally intense situation.

Slavery to the perceptions and projections of the emotions fades as the heart is cleansed. Love is no longer used as a weapon or a punishment. Since we have already realized the grandness of creation, we know that other people are not responsible for our emotions. Love is no longer seen as a commodity that requires us to negotiate, manipulate, and terrorize others to procure. We come to realize that all the Love we need comes from the source of creation. This Love is literally all around us. Like a fish that swims in water, we live, move, and breathe in a world where everything vibrates with Love.

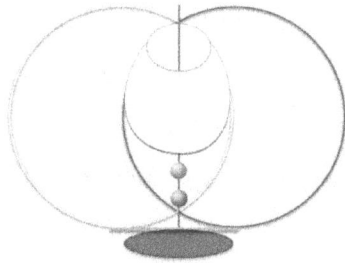

The next area of our lives to come into focus is the seat of our personal power. Personal empowerment is not about controlling others or imposing our will on everything that is going on around us. When you take control of your personal situation, you are building self-respect, self-worth, and confidence. Up until this point all thoughts and actions were directed toward giving to others. We now add a layer that includes "*Me.*" In the matrix of life, we cannot forget ourselves. There is a big difference between being a servant and being a slave. The servant chooses the situations and circumstances that they wish to participate in and which they do not. A slave has no choice and is haphazardly blown about by the demands of others. The difference between these two points of view is as simple as a shift in attitude. When we consciously choose to give, then thoughts of being taken advantage of cannot emerge or will fade away quickly.

Accepting the consequences of your current life and taking responsibility for the things that will make it better is the first step to empowering yourself. It's time to stop wishing and start doing. Begin small. Schedule times for getting a couple of chores done. As you are able to regularly accomplish these chores, add additional things to your roster. Designate locations for commonly used items and return these items to their designated locations. That way you will have what you need, when you need it.

Choosing who, what, when, and where to give requires the discipline to say, "NO." At this time, we realize that we are human and have physical limitations of time and resources. We must accept that we cannot be everything to everyone. It is important to create a hierarchy of priority. Here is where we decide who and what gets our time, attention, and money. Allowing a low priority relationship to suck the life out of you to the point where you cannot provide for the needs in your highest priority group is a sign that they need to go. When this happens, start cutting or limiting the people and activities that generate excess anxiety, never-ending strife, or exhaustion. Then, ruthlessly stick to that plan.

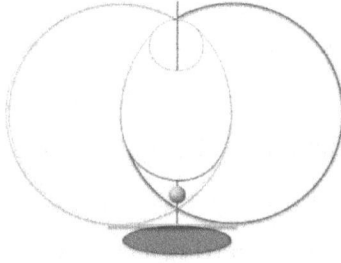

The sixth attainment along the Water Path pertains to removing desires. We each have minor compulsions and addictions that have become substitutes for love or joy. Here, we learn that the greatest pleasure that life can offer comes when our entire being is in balance. Balance cannot be achieved through fighting. It can only be achieved through awareness and acceptance. We find that fighting our bad habits increases their hold on us. The reason is that stress and fighting increases the Fire energy in the bioelectrical system, which causes an increase in desire. Instead of battling those pesky compulsions, the way to wholeness is to increase the Water energy. Washing the inner being with Water and Light will cause those habits to whither and eventually fade over time. The deeper you go within, more and more Water energy is needed maintain the attainments. When we forget to man the pumps that bring down the Water energy, those irritating addictions will come back and haunt us.

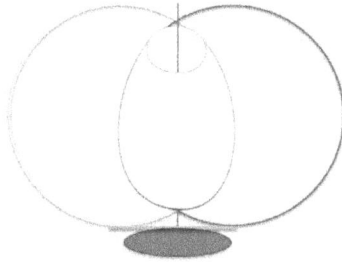

It is possible to reach a point where even the most basic need of food and water ceases. Saints and sages that understand the workings of the bioelectrical field can go extended periods of time without eating or drinking because the Water energy is able to fulfill all the bodily needs. Connecting the Water energy to the ground is the next attainment. Struggle ends and we experience the Peace that passes all understanding. Once the circuit is firmly connected, the flow of the cosmic energies circulates freely. In this chakra, the needs of security are addressed. We come to know that the universe operates in mysterious ways that are always giving us what we need in the moment. There is always enough and we will always be provided for. It allows us to enjoy life no matter where we are or what circumstances we find ourselves.

Once the cleansing of the entire inner being is complete, the aura is filled with a glowing white light. The ancient Egyptians referred to this attainment as the *white robe*. The Christian tradition calls this attainment the *transfiguration*. The white lotus on which the Buddha sits symbolizes the encircling energy that defines this attainment. The gnostic terminology for this same achievement is the *Cosmic Egg*.

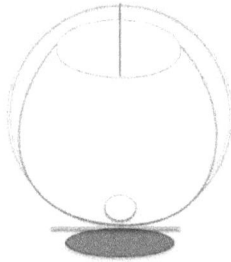

Once the desires are quelled, continued practice will produce an excess of Water energy that will pool in the lower abdomen. With time and continued practice, the excess Water energy will coalesce and grow. The mind's eye will interpret this event as a white pearl, a white stone, or the planting of a seed. A woman will have the tendency to interpret this event as a pregnancy because the movement of the energies through the belly truly feels like the kicking of a fetus in the womb. Since the Water energy is masculine, the divine child that is created is always male. This is the birth of the masculine qualities of logic, order, and discipline, within the psyche. In Jungian terms, this is the emergence of the animus within a woman. As we said before, the Taoist *The Secret of the Golden Flower* and the Christian *Nativity Story* recount the process of this transformation.

As you can see, the Fire energy is never allowed to rise within the bioelectrical field of the soul. The "sword that kills the innocent babe in the womb" is not allowed rise. When we use the more intimate metaphors for the rise of the Fire energy, we can see why a practitioner of this path would be called a perpetual "virgin." The titles given to those who complete this path are *The Virgin Queen, The Queen of Heaven,* or *The Star.*

MYSTICAL LAW #4 - THE ARCHETYPES OF LUCIFER AND SATAN

Today, the names Lucifer and Satan are considered interchangeable, but that was not always so. The ancient cultures that honored both energies understood that there were two ways to wholeness and two ways to destruction. The Water that was a blessing that grew crops could also become a flood that destroyed everything. The Fire that brought warmth and a well-cooked meal can become uncontrollable and burn down an entire city.

In their stories, the ancient cultures created archetypes that depicted the typical behaviors of people whose energy system was unbalanced. The ancients believed that men were born with the Water, or masculine energy, as dominant. While women, were born with the Fire, or feminine energy, as dominant. Imbalance ensues when more of the dominant energy is poured into the spiritual system.

Creative personalities, who underwent the initiation of the Fire energy, became crazed and violent. The expanding energy widened the mind to the point of chaos. They were described as being possessed by demons. Their anger and sexual promiscuity was legendary. In patriarchal societies, this deepened the prejudice against women. Since the initiations caused a majority of women to become maniacs instead of making them better people, it lead to the belief that women were spiritually incompetent. Women were then banned from spiritual leadership and later relegated to the level of second-class citizen because they could not endure the initiation of the Fire energies.

Intellectual personalities, who underwent the empowerment of the Water energy, became more judgmental and critical. The contracting energy made them arrogant and hardened their opinions.

These men then felt that they had a right to destroy anything that did not fit into their philosophy. These men were feared by all and many cultures instituted mandatory initiations of Fire energy to prevent any man from becoming a menace to society.

In the Christian Bible, Lucifer is found only in the first chapter of Genesis. *The Fall of Lucifer* is the only story we find. Scholars have determined that the first book of the Torah is an amalgamation of the ancient oral tradition that was finally written down. *The Fall of Lucifer* marks the beginning of the merging of these two evil archetypes. When God the Father became the One True God and the Light became all good, it was not logical to have two evil entities within the theological structure. In later chapters, the evil entity is referred to only as Satan. As time progresses toward the present era, Satan was transformed from a woman to a man. The properties of arrogance and unbridled desires are merged into one character. Over time, these depictions have evolved and mutated into the theologies of today. We will use the most ancient traditions to reformulate the archetypes of Lucifer and Satan, since the original meanings have been blended through time. We will not go into great depth. We will just outline the basics of these two archetypes.

SATAN

The Satan archetype is the blend of the creative and emotional personality with an over abundance of the Divine Feminine energy of Fire. An individual who prefers the creative circuit of the brain, most likely, has Fire as the dominant energy in their bioelectrical system. As we learned above, the Fire energy is an expanding energy. It opens the mind to all possibility. When we increase the amount of Fire energy in a creative personality, it makes a person who already has trouble staying focused even more scatter-brained. This combination of personal warmth with Fire leads to bursts of anger and unquenchable desires.

In ancient times, this archetype was always depicted as an evil woman. The pantheon of deities in most cultures included the Dr. Jekyll and Mr. Hyde depictions of the goddess. The loving mother goddess was widely known for her ability to turn into the goddess of death and destruction. In ancient Egypt, the loving mother goddess was Hathor and the destructive goddess was Sekhmet. In Hindu culture, the loving mother goddess is Shakti and the manifestation of death and destruction is the goddess Kali. In the Christian theology, we find this same combination of Queen of Heaven and Demon possessed prostitute in the characters of Mother Mary and Mary Magdalene.

There are several historical representations of women whose emotions became ablaze with destruction. We begin with the story of the Celtic Queen Boudicca. She lived during the early Roman occupation of Britain. She was married to a Celtic king who reigned over the Iceni tribe. In order to keep the Iceni tribe in tact, King Prasutagus, peacefully annexed the tribe to Roman rule. Upon the death of the king, the tribe's nobles elected their queen, Boudicca, to the supreme leadership of the tribe. The Roman legions became offended because women were not allowed to have leadership positions according to Roman law. When the tribe refused to vote a man to lead them, Rome retaliated. They enslaved all the nobles and confiscated their lands and property. Tacitus tells us that Boudicca was publically flogged and her daughters were publically raped in her sight in order to force submission to Roman rule. Instead of gaining her submission, the harsh treatment incited Boudicca to lead a rebellion.

Boudicca's band of rebels assaulted and destroyed all three Roman garrisons on the Isle of Britton, which included Londinium, today's London. The rebel force was so great that the commander of Londinium's garrison had to abandon Londinium to the rebels, who promptly burnt it to the ground. As with other settlements, the rebels slaughtered everyone who had not evacuated with the legions. It is estimated that Boudicca's band of rebels killed 70,000-80,000 people in the destruction of Rome's three garrisons. In the end, tactical strategy won out over unbridled rage. Boudicca's band of rebels were finally out maneuvered by the one remaining Roman legion that had been away from their garrison at the time of Boudicca's attack. The stories from the ancient historians differ. So, we will never know if Boudicca was killed in battle or if she killed herself to prevent capture and further humiliation. Her rage and subsequent destruction of three Roman garrisons is reminiscent of the Hindu parable of Kali whose thirst for blood was so great that the King of the Gods had to put her to sleep to stop the violence.

Pliny writes of another historical example of the destructive female archetype. Valeria Messalina, the third wife of emperor Claudius, was portrayed as extremely licentious. There is an oft-repeated tale that Messalina competed in a sexual marathon against one of Rome's leading prostitutes. Pliny records the competition as lasting 24 hours, which Messalina won with the score of 25 partners. It is said that even after this extraordinary number of sexual encounters, Messalina went home unsatisfied.

LUCIFER

The Lucifer archetype is the blend of an intellectual personality with an over abundance of the Divine Masculine energy of Water. An individual that prefers the executive function circuit in the brain, most likely, has Water as the dominant energy in their energy system. As we learned above, Water is a contracting energy. It hardens the mind's perceptions and judgments. It turns a person who is prone to prejudice into a fanatic. Those who do not fit within the norms of their philosophy can illicit a variety of responses that ranges from personal disgust to considering them to be unworthy of life.

This archetype fits the modern definition of a psychopath. There is no true warmth for humanity in those who possess this personality type. It is so outside the norm of social interaction that we call this a personality disorder. These people think only of themselves. They associate with only those that they can manipulate to provide them with what they want. The most accomplished have learned skills that project the perception of caring, which they then turn against their victims.

Lucifer is the archetype of the evil king. He is an arrogant man, who thinks only of himself, and uses his power solely for his personal benefit.

MYSTICAL LAW #5 – BREATH AND THOUGHT MOVE THE ENERGIES

The bioelectrical field is sublime. It takes time and practice to sense these, normally unnoticeable, energies within your being. The reason for this is that the breath and the thought govern the movement of the energies. For the most part, we are not aware of our breathing. In order to have control of the circulation of the bioelectrical energies, the breath must be trained.

Over time, our breathing becomes tangled into knots causing us to inhale shallowly from the chest, which limits the power of our breathing. When we breathe this way, we barely get enough oxygen to serve the body's cells. There is nothing left to circulate the energies. The first order of business is to retrain your breathing so that each breath flows deeply down into the belly. Watch an infant as it breathes. Notice how their belly fully expands with each breath. Breathing the way that nature intended will energize you. Since the breath is also linked to the body's autonomic system, taking deep breaths will reduce stress and bring calmness.

As we learned in the previous chapter, how you breathe determines which energy is boosted in your bioelectrical system. In general, when you breathe in through the nose and out through the mouth, the Water energy is increased. Take time to notice how this way of breathing intensifies the fall of the Water energy. It calms the mind and brings Peace. With practice, you will be able to connect this energy, which originates in the sky, to the ground. Once connected, the Peace you feel in the depth of your being is miraculous. Christians call this, "The Peace that passes understanding."

When you breathe through the mouth and out through the nose, the Fire energy is activated. This type of breathing brings up the emotions. It forces us to see the wider view of our behaviors. We begin to see that when our focus is strictly on ourselves, we hurt others. Love and compassion are natural side effects when the mind is inclusive and is open to all possibility. With practice, you will be able to connect this energy, which is derived from the ground, to the sky. Once connected, you will have access to the expanse of the divine.

These are just the basics. Both the Taoist and the Hindu traditions have mastered many ways to manipulate the breath. Breathing through just one nostril, counting the seconds of inhale verses the seconds of exhale, and pumping the diaphragm are just a few of the thousands of possible breath practices. The qi gong and yogic traditions are not just stretching exercises. The stretches do little in and of themselves. The goal is to manipulate the body so that specific energy channels are opened and connected. When you add breathing to these practices, it pushes energy through these opened channels. It is when you coordinate the breath with the exercises that true advancement takes place.

The other method of manipulating the bioelectrical energies is to use thought. In order for the thought to guide the energies, the mind must be clear of issues. It must be trained not to get involved in judging the random events of the day or continually chattering on about subjects that no longer concern your current circumstance. For those who consider meditation to be the manipulation of the bioelectrical energies, true meditation cannot take place until the mind can be brought to silence.

Once the mind is silent, the imagination is trained to direct the bioelectrical energies. Training begins as a practice that is performed only during formal meditation. The mind is gently redirected to the object of focus every time it wanders. Over time, this trains the mind to stay focused on the intended task. As you advance, you learn that it is possible to practice anytime and anywhere. It is good to check in on the movement of the energies running through your bioelectrical field periodically throughout the day. Take a moment while waiting in line at the store to scan your energy system. Are you breathing properly? How is the energy flowing? Do you need to change the direction the energies are flowing? Are there places in your body that are dark or feel a lack of energy? If so, address these issues with some focused attention and deep belly breaths.

Mind training can use anything. Simple nature scenes, complex images of gods or goddesses, and reconstructing mechanisms are just a few of the ways to train the imagination. The goal is to stay on task. So, if you are squeamish about using religious symbols and icons, don't worry. It does not matter if you visualize sitting in the lap of Father Sky enfolded in the clouds of his essence or if you visualize the energy of Water or Light streaming down through the top of your head all the way down to your toes. Either visualization will train the mind to stay on task and move the energy in the proper direction.

MYSTICAL LAW #6 – *WATER BRINGS FIRE AND FIRE BRINGS WATER*

In our world, the sun rises as the moon sets. The continual motion of the cosmos instigates never-ending change. The pendulum is constantly swinging from one extreme to the other extreme only to return and repeat the cycle again. We find these cycles in each day, in each year, and in each progression of the equinox. The ebb and flow of the energies within the mystical energy system is also in continual motion. Our lives govern the patterns of energy that move through our bodies. We can open our awareness of the energies and help them to flow or we can allow the stresses of our lives to unbalance our bioelectrical field and cause distress and disease.

The process of spiritual development begins with cleansing the system. None of us begins this process with a clean slate. We all have our past history and issues to sift through. It is not possible to clean grease with more grease. When we ramp up the Fire energy in a person who primarily uses the imagination circuit of the brain and is not in control of their emotions, the result is a crazed and angry being. When we ramp up the Water energy in an intellectual person who primarily uses the executive function circuit and is already critical and judgmental, we create a person that becomes so dogmatic that they can justify the abuse of others.

The energy that will cut through the accumulated sludge in our spiritual systems is the latent energy. This means that the energy that you will use to cleanse the bioelectrical field will be dependent upon which energy is dominant in your bioelectrical field. If you are predominately intellectual, then the latent energy that will, most likely, cleanse your spiritual system is Fire. If you are predominantly creative or emotional, then the latent energy that will, most likely, wash your spiritual system is Water.

Once cleansed, the dominant energy will return and fill the entire space. This second return unleashes a pure energy that is not contaminated with issues or past events. The blend of the two energies creates a balanced state. The Christian tradition uses the metaphor, "The Water turns to Wine" and "The return of Jesus," to describe this mystical event. Those who are intellectual will experience "The Flood" or "Enlightenment."

Once the energies have reached a balance, it is possible to intensify or raise your spiritual state. The way that this is done is to continue to gradually increase the latent energy. This will pump more of the pure dominant energy into your energy system. It is a stair-step method. It is important not to go too far or too fast. Working too hard or too fast can put your spiritual system at risk of imbalance and annihilation. So, do as scuba divers do. Go slowly. Take time out to plateau and allow the energies to balance themselves before continuing on your way.

MYSTICAL LAW #7 - WATER AND FIRE ANNIHILATE EACH OTHER

The energies of Water and Fire can be likened to matter and anti-matter. It is not possible or wise to mix these two energies. Oil and water peacefully separate when mixed. When Water and Fire are brought together, they annihilate each other, in an explosive manner. If you have seen the movie *Angels and Demons*, there is a scene where the scientist explains how a small amount of anti-matter when it comes into contact with matter creates not just a huge explosion but an annihilation. When this happens, all energy, both the dominant and the latent energy, is reduced to almost nothing.

When both energies of the bioelectrical field are reduced to almost nothing, the brain is unable to function properly. The synapsis cannot hum and the mental state is reduced to overwhelming confusion and abject hopelessness. Hopefully, you will never experience this form of absolute desperation and despair. But if you do, know that it is possible to rise again from the ashes if you return to your practices and gently work to rebuild all the energy that was destroyed.

When more of your dominant energy is poured into your bioelectrical field, before the latent energy can complete the job of cleansing the inner being, it overloads all the circuits and explodes. It can be metaphorically described as a blown fuse or pouring diesel fuel into a gasoline engine. Too much Fire will boil away all the Water in the system and too much Water will completely douse the Fire energy. This can cause memory erasure that runs from partial memory loss of a day to a couple of weeks and can even cause a complete wiping of all memory. I have heard of cases where the person involved experienced a complete erasure of their memory after an energy healer "balanced" her energy. Not only did they have to relearn their name and personal history, their memory was returned an infantile state and they had to relearn everything, including how to feed, walk, and toilet themselves.

I have personally experienced the state of annihilation on more than one occasion. It is something that I would not wish upon my worst enemy. The reason why I am so passionate about this topic is because none of the spiritual teachers that caused the anguish in my spiritual system did so out of meanness or as a method to maliciously control me. They truly thought they were advancing my spiritual development. However, every one of them was ignorant of the basic principles of mysticism. Even the most educated of my teachers, did not know that there were two transformative spiritual energies and that these two very different energies were the basis for two very different paths to wholeness.

Annihilation is the reason behind why we find religion-based strife from the beginning of time until the present. Under normal circumstance, when someone has experienced this type of distress, they will blame the person who did this to them. It is a natural response to hate and lash out against those who harmed you. In the most extreme cases, whole groups will go on the warpath to have everyone change to their preferred belief system or to have the injurious religion eradicated completely. When a whole community accepts one energy as holy and the other energy as evil, the twin paths to wholeness are reduced to one. When this happens, half of the population is denied access to the practices that will bring them to energetic balance and advanced personal development.

There are many who currently believe that the solution to this problem is to eradicate religion all together. Abolition of religion was tried, most recently, by the communist state. However, it did not exterminate religion. As in the past, the spiritual traditions went underground and waited until conditions improved before reemerging. Since religion is a result of the natural energy phenomenon associated with this planet, it cannot be eliminated. The better solution is to return religion to its former status as the science of consciousness. We have come to a point in time when we are on the verge of constructing a universal scientific paradigm that brings unity to the diverse cultural metaphors, parables, and myths.

MYSTICAL LAW #8 - KNOW THYSELF

Knowing yourself is the next law in mysticism. It is not possible for you to take charge of your personal development when you do not understand yourself. Knowing your personality type, what issues you carry, and which energy is dominant in your spiritual system gives you valuable knowledge that can help you make wise spiritual choices. You will be able to discern for yourself which practices are beneficial and which practices are harmful to your energy system. When you know yourself, you will also have the basic knowledge needed to evaluate a spiritual teacher or guide. Instead of being fully dependent upon a spiritual teacher, you will have the knowledge to partner with your guide. When you can provide detailed insight to your teacher, they are better able to recommend practices that will swiftly and easily move you to higher levels of attainment. Blindly believing in a spiritual teacher is the most common mistake of a new mystic that, in some cases, can lead to disastrous results.

The first step to spiritual development is to spend some time performing a series of self-evaluations. Participating in personality tests, like the Myers-Briggs or Enneagram, can be very insightful. They will give you multiple ways to see yourself. Also, spend time everyday watching yourself and recording everything that took place during your day in a journal. When you read your journal later, notice what you noticed and what you left out. Was the focus of your writing very narrow? What did you concentrate on? Were you worried more about yourself or others? Were you describing feelings and perceptions or ideas and concepts? Was your writing very linear or did you forget pieces in the middle? Were you able to stick to one theme or did you wander off topic? Do you have a tendency to be creative or intellectual? It does not matter how you accomplish this step. What matters is that you complete it first. Don't be afraid of what you find. There is no right or wrong. Awareness is your goal. Once you are aware, you can change.

Make a habit of testing out various practices before you jump in with both feet. Start with only five-minute sessions. Spiritual practices are like exercise. If you do too much on the first day, you will suffer with the equivalent of sore muscles. Notice how you think, feel, and behave after participating in a particular practice. Keep diligent records of your experiences and progress. Be aware that spiritual practices will bring up past issues that can be uncomfortable. You can lower the intensity of the practice, but keep going with that practice until the issue is cleared. If a practice causes true distress, such as extreme mental confusion or excessive judgment, <u>stop that practice immediately.</u>

MYSTICAL LAW #9 - KNOW THY PATH AND KNOW THY STUDENT

Once you have reached an advanced level of personal development, it is now possible for you to guide others. In order for you to do this, you will need to become educated. Not everyone develops in the same way or will benefit from same methods that brought you to your state of development. Your education needs to cover all the methods that can benefit your future students. *Be aware that even with all this study, you will know and understand only one of the two spiritual paths.*

The law of Knowing Thyself is especially important for those who guide others along the spiritual path. Not only do you need to become aware of yourself, but you will also need to understand the needs of your student(s). It is natural to think that everyone will do well following the same path and doing the same practices that you did. This kind of thinking is problematic because each person is unique and there are two distinctly different paths of personal development. If you force someone, who is incompatible with your path, to follow in your footsteps, you will instigate imbalance in their energy matrix. This can do serious damage to your student's physical health and mental wellbeing.

This is why it is so very important that you evaluate each student as a unique person. As a spiritual teacher or guide, there are a great number of personality testing methods available to you. Evaluation can be accomplished in either a casual or professional fashion and can include multiple-choice tests, free associations, and general observation. Your first order of business is to determine which path this student needs to take. Do not make the same mistake the ancients made and assume that all males should follow the Fire Path and all females should follow the Water Path. Evaluate each person individually and recommend the appropriate practices for their individual needs.

You should NEVER, NEVER, NEVER initiate or manipulate the energy of anyone that you have not fully evaluated AND found to be compatible with your school of development.

Until you have traveled and completed the other path, DO NOT accept any student that requires the other path to evolve. Rejecting a student that is incompatible with your style of teaching is the most compassionate thing you can do for them. Explain to them why you are not the best choice for them and refer these students to a qualified teacher of the appropriate path.

MYSTICAL LAW #10 - *SPIRITUAL TEXTS AND SYMBOLS ARE SCIENTIFIC FORMULAS*

The mystical texts are not just make-believe stories fashioned to entertain an audience. They were not created as accurate historical documentation, either. There is a specific purpose for mystical texts. They were created to explain the principles and laws of the bioelectrical field of the soul. They are what I call caveman physics because they explain the phenomenon of the bioelectrical field in pre-scientific terms.

The ancients did not have advanced mathematics or physics to explain the mystical phenomenon. They used stories and pictures to pass along the information. From the caves in France that were painted over 40,000 years ago to the Ox pictures of the Tao, these pictures and stories are still with us today. Describing the experience of the bioelectrical field is as varied as the number of people who have lived on this planet. What is missing is the unifying principles in which to interpret the teachings. The ancients knew that if you followed the recipe that was outlined in the pictures and stories, you would achieve a higher level of personal development. This means that the spiritual texts are actually scientific formulas.

The fundamental truths of the bioelectrical field of the soul have traditionally been explained by using diverse metaphorical symbols and relationships. Since science has not named the spiritual energies, as yet, our only method of explaining the physics and chemistry of the bioelectrical field is to follow in the footsteps of the ancients and use metaphor. The metaphors come from a wide range of human experience. The stories can incorporate processes of nature such as a sunrise or the process of pollination. They can include human relationships such as war, marriage, or sex. They can be very simple or extremely complex.

For instance, Rain is one of the many metaphorical symbols for the energy that falls from the sky. The reason "Rain" was chosen is because the properties of the Water energy match many of the properties of rain. It is Water. It is clear. It is cooling. It falls from the sky. It cleanses. It makes the seeds sprout and grow into food. For those who live in hot, dry climates, it is a blessing from above. Water and Rain are not the only ways to describe the process of spiritual development that uses the energy that falls from above. The process of pollination and bearing fruit as well as the process of pregnancy and birth are other ways to describe the exact same process. While historical events might be the basis of a metaphor, it is important to look deeper than historical fact. We are seeking to find the scientific formula that defines the bioelectrical framework, which was the true purpose of the mystical author.

Let's take for example the earliest known spiritual text, *The Epic of Gilgamesh*. It is the spiritual journey of an ego-encrusted king. It is the oldest known tale that uses the Hero's Journey as its format. When you understand that the monster he finds is his ego and the sex scenes with the temple priestess represent the initiation of the Fire energy, you are well on your way to understanding the energy processes that bring spiritual transformation. The final chapters of the story contain the return of the dominant energy, Water, in the form of a flood. This text is quite amazing because it proves that the knowledge of the bioelectrical field, in relation to the spiritual journey of an egoistic personality, was fully fleshed out well over 5,000 years ago. This journey is universal in all cultures, throughout time. That is why many of the principles and concepts for transformation are the same from culture to culture throughout recorded history.

In many ancient cultures, we find that it was believed that the men must awaken before sunrise so that they can sing the sun into existence each day. We modern humans scoff at such beliefs. In our scientific age, we are able to watch our planet spin on its axis from satellites and see how this causes the cycle of night into day. We moderns find such beliefs nothing more than superstition. In our minds, we are thinking, "What kind of crazy thinks that they have the power to determine whether the sun rises each morning when the rising of the sun is a scientific fact related to the rotation of the earth on its axis?"

But, what if the ancient and indigenous peoples were not talking literally about the rise of the sun that brings day to our planet? Could it be possible that they were metaphorically describing the rise of the Fire energy within their own bioelectrical field? If so, then, these peoples are performing the same practices that are found in monastic communities throughout time and around the globe. It is not uncommon for monks and nuns of many different faiths to rise before dawn to start their daily prayer cycles. These practices follow the cycle of the energies and are designed to bring the practitioner into alignment with the universal forces.

These cycles are not just singular circles. The cycles of life are intensely complex and interwoven. The Mayan culture is not the only culture to document the interwoven cycles of time. The priests of the Catholic faith also incorporate daily, seasonally, and multi-year remembrances, like Jubilee, which is celebrated once every twenty-five years, into their worship routines. The Chinese tradition incorporates a twelve-year cycle of years. These years are depicted as twelve different animals, which are, then again, subdivided into the five elements. This means that if you are born into the year of the Fire Dragon it will be sixty years before that exact elemental animal will return.

The requirements for energy upkeep are different depending upon each faith's beliefs. Islam requires its followers to worship five times a day, while the Catholic faith requires its followers to worship once a week and on special holy days. In many faiths, only the priests and spiritual experts are required to perform daily worship. In these cultures, it was the spiritual leaders who kept the energies balanced for the entire community. In some cases, small groups of spiritual specialists, like the six Vestal Virgins of ancient Rome, were considered enough to keep the energies balanced for the entire empire. We may consider such beliefs nothing more than outrageous imagination but scientific studies are showing that groups of meditators can actually change the crime rate in the area surrounding their meditation site.

CONCLUSION

These ten laws formulate the basic structure of mysticism. How this structure is used and interpreted differs from culture to culture. Some honored the Fire energy and specialized in the ways to enhance and increase this energy within the bioelectrical matrix. Other cultures revered the Water energy. Their myths and symbols educated the population on the ways of bringing Peace to the inner being. These differences, along with the cultural distinctions, are why the integrated framework of spiritual development has remained hidden for so long.

It is only through compiling the evidence from many spiritual belief systems that the commonalities coalesce into a framework that is all-inclusive.

CONCLUSION

I have tried to divide an integrated system into its component parts. Such divisions make it easier to come to grips with the basics of mysticism. However, the reality is that all these parts are interrelated and a shift in any one facet affects all the others. With this understanding, it is easy to see that each person is a unique expression of a unified field that contains an innumerable number of variables. There are no repeats in persons or in individual experience. The only tenant that can be touted to all those who wish to journey along the mystical path is *Balance*.

In order to create balance, you must, "Know Thyself." You must determine your starting point before you begin this journey, because the way to the destination varies and is dependent upon each person's starting point. You must also be willing to walk through the fire of change, even when it does not feel good. Your head will ache while new circuitry is being blazed into your brain. Your perceptions will be shattered when you see that in truth everything you are feeling is just a concoction of chemicals that are put into motion based on your past experiences. Your expectations of others will die when you realize that your experience has nothing to do with their action and everything to do with how you control your chemistry and perceptions.

You will find that there is no end to practice. There is no moment when you can say you are "*done.*" It is important to keep the bioelectrical energies in constant motion to both transform the spirit and to sustain a specific level of personal development. This journey will never be boring because once you have achieved a pinnacle of development, another challenge will appear on the next horizon.

The depth of mystical mastery will be determined by the extent of the mystic's ability to control all facets of the body-mind-spirit complex. Since the number of variables in the equation of spiritual development is innumerable, there is no end to the possible things that you can learn to control.

Once the lessons of the bioelectrical field are fully understood by the general population, the changes to the social order of our planet will be as wide spread as when the idea of interchangeable parts came to manufacturing. Many fields will be irrevocability changed. It is obvious that religion will be the first to experience the changes. Once the majority of people understand that religion is a system of personal development that is geared to a specific personality type, religions will specialize in teaching only those who possess that specific personality type. There will be entrance exams that will include personality typing, brain circuitry mapping, and brain frequency tests in addition to the knowledge level that is required today. The most elite mystics will be those who can lead anyone to expanded awareness. They will have the ability to teach not just the students who follow the method of development that brought them to enlightenment, but also the students of the opposite path as well.

War and strife that is based on religious ideals and principles would come to a screeching halt. The goal of humanity would be to become as highly developed as possible. Instead of forcing everyone to believe that your religion is the best for everyone, the emphasis will be on finding which religion is best for you and your developmental potential. The actual religion or spiritual progenitor you follow will no longer matter.

We will have a system of spiritual understanding that is comprised of twin energies that are mutually dependent upon each other. Women will again have access to a spiritual system that brings balance to their bioelectrical fields and have the ability to participate in personal development as well as attain spiritual leadership positions.

We will no longer see young children indoctrinated into a religion simply because it was the church that their family has attended for generations. I foresee a time when school children will be taught the basic breathing practices and the school day will include a 30-minute session of yoga or tai chi style exercise. Lessons will be geared to balancing the brain's circuits and music will be used to develop the harmonic frequencies of the mind. The interpretation of the spiritual scriptures will be seen as recipes for developing and changing the human bioelectrical field and not historical fact.

The study of ancient peoples and archeology will no longer be a jumble of strange artifacts and weird practices. It will become clear why the ancients did what they did. We will know why they considered these practices so important that they left artifacts in graves, clues in the artwork of the culture, and evidence in the myths and stories they created. We will be able categorize each belief system in a way that helps us determine the best path for each person. Their writings will be used in modern practical ways instead of being displayed as oddities in museums to be gawked at by those who don't have a deep understanding of the sophisticated theories and methodologies that these texts contain.

The sciences of the body and brain are currently studying the spiritual practices and their elite practitioners. The early findings are remarkable and scientifically repeatable. For better, or for worse, we will be able to mass-produce spiritually enlightened humans. We will be mapping the religions and societal belief systems in a way that designates which energy was primarily honored so that we can designate which system of personal development will bring the greatest beneficial change to each individual. No longer will there be the random few who benefit from the process of spiritual development. We will then come into an age of human existence that is compassionate to all living things and is at peace with the different spiritual philosophies.

Last but not least, the science of physics could also be affected because that which is within is also without. It could be possible that the nature of the positive and negative forces that create the physical matter of the human body could be used on a universal scale. I predict that Star Trek's medical tricorders, which are just vibrational healing machines, and food replicators will be a part of our everyday lives in the very near future. I'm sure that there is so much more but, like all people, my mind is limited. So, this is all that my little mind can envision at this time. I can only hope that I live to see the new beginnings that will come to our world when these understandings start to take hold in a significant part of the population.

ABOUT THE AUTHOR

Mischa V Alyea is a jack-of-all-trades and loves all things ecological and environmental. She has done everything from developing an inventing workshop as the elementary science fair coordinator, to directing Day Camp for 300 girls, to refinishing the wood floors in her home. She is an accomplished seamstress, event planner, DIY'er, and cat herder.

Mischa got her first real taste of religion when she spent a brief time as a Catholic. She was confirmed in 1984, but soon after left the church. It was fourteen years before she again looked into the teachings of the church. In 1998, Mischa was introduced to meditation when she joined Unity. It was at this time that she became deeply interested in religion, psychology, and spiritual practice. It was here that she delved deeply into the Christian religion. Later, she was initiated into Sufism and empowered by a Tibetan Rinpoche. She furthered her studies by reading the works of the mystics, as well as studied, Buddhism, Taoism, and Zen. When she was introduced to the practice of Qi Gong, her interests turned to energy practice and theory.

As the founder of Aashni Spiritual Living, Mischa writes and publishes books on meditation and integrated spiritual philosophy. Mischa lives in Kansas City with her husband Tom and Sushi the infamous *House Monster*.

Aashni
Spiritual Living

Visit us at:

www.AashniSpiritualLiving.com

Also by
Mischa V Alyea

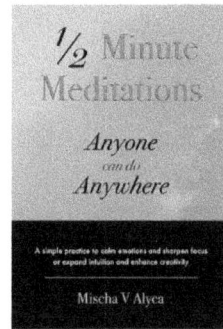

Visit our website for a complete listing

www.AashniSpiritualliving.com